Build Therefore Your Own World

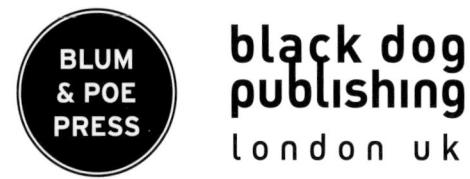

BLUM & POE PRESS

black dog publishing
london uk

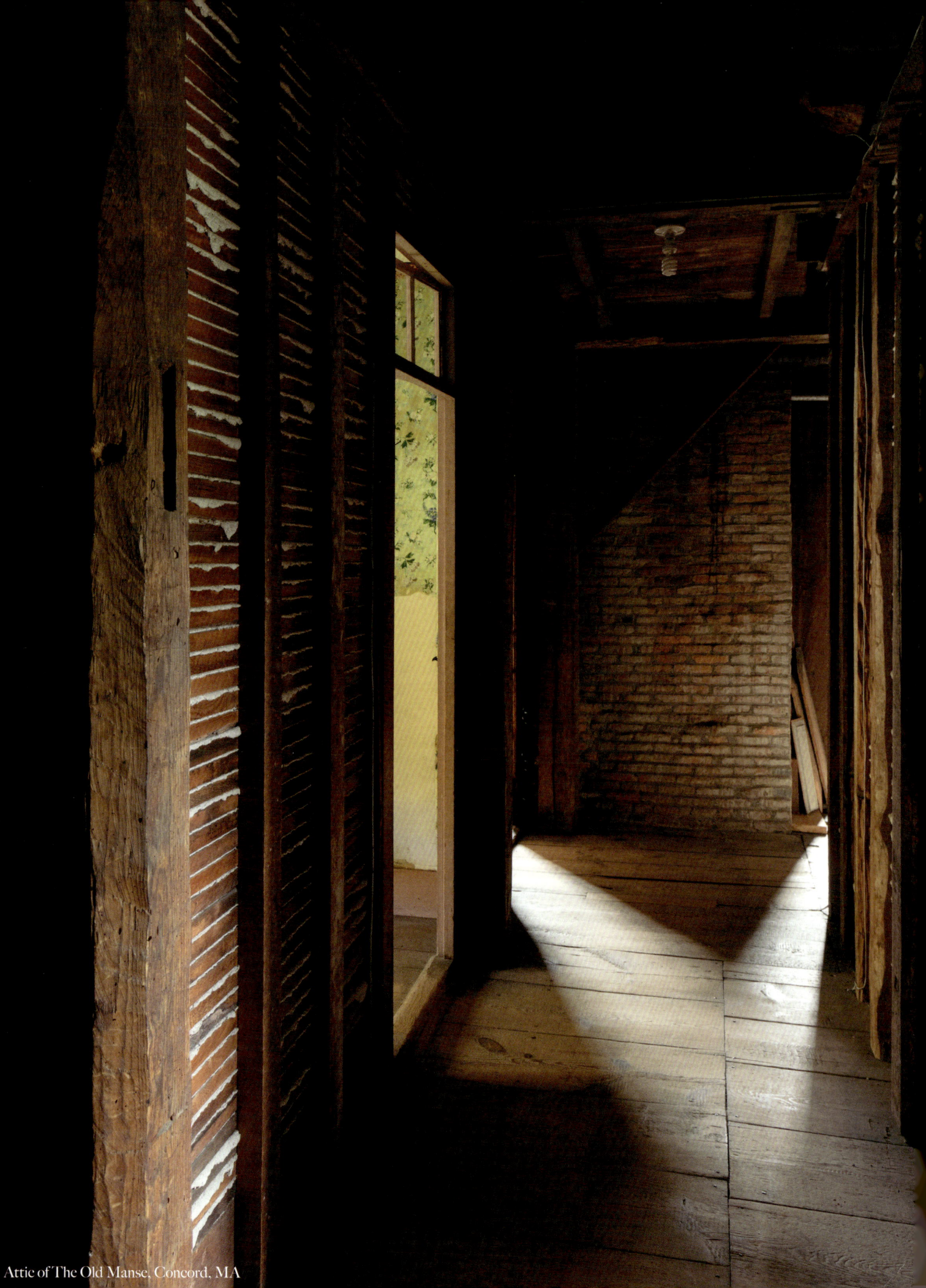

Attic of The Old Manse, Concord, MA

Sam Durant

3

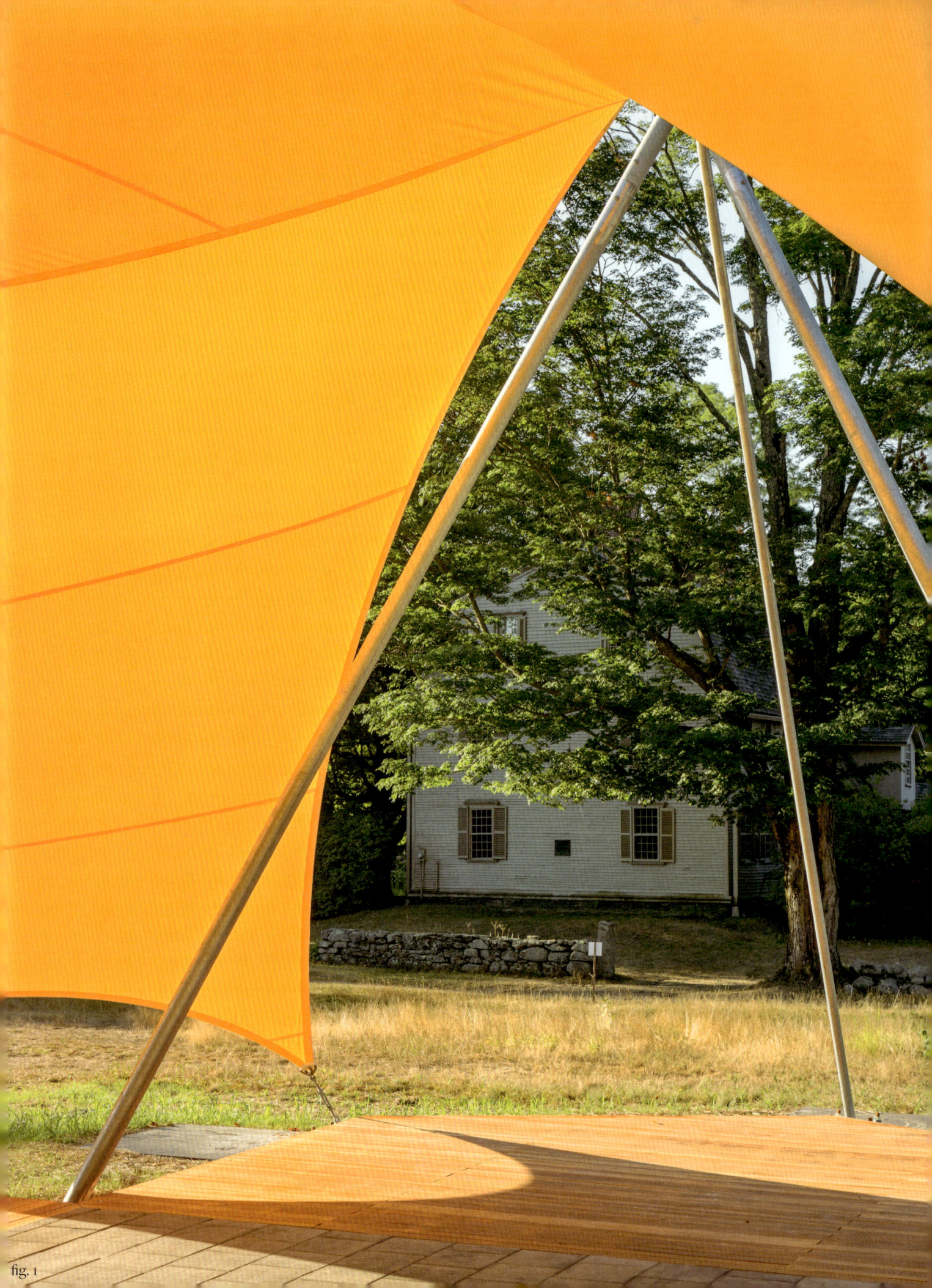

fig. 1

Suburban Hymn:

Complacency = Complicity

Pedro Alonzo

In his research-based practice, Sam Durant follows a tradition of radical historians and writers such as Howard Zinn, Roxanne Dunbar-Ortiz, Robin D. G. Kelley, Ward Churchill, and Elise Lemire. Inspired by their work, Durant uncovers aspects of history that have remained largely unknown to mainstream society. Some of Durant's previous projects include a demystification of the origin myths of Plymouth Rock and Thanksgiving, and highlighting the human and economic costs of mass incarceration. He sees this work as critical in order to acknowledge the past and strive for the future that the American Revolution and the civil rights movement promised. His work on the historic site of The Old Manse in Concord, Massachusetts, entitled *The Meeting House* (2016) (fig. 1), looks at the legacy of slavery and its continuing role in the systemic forms of racism we face today.

The Meeting House proposes the uncomfortable idea that veiled and institutional forms of racism were largely developed in the North and continue to thrive today through the complacency or complicity of whites. Durant stated in an interview that:

> African-Americans experience discrimination and worse every day, they don't need to be informed about this. It is the minds and hearts of whites that need to be opened, they are the primary audience for *The Meeting House*.[1]

Three of Durant's previous artworks are notable in this lineage of commemorating the subjugated and pointing to the correlating white supremacist hegemony. In *Proposal for White and Indian Dead Monument Transpositions* (2005), the artist recreated a series of monuments erected to commemorate the massacre of indigenous people during the colonization of North America (fig. 2).[2]

The stone obelisks are representative of policies of betrayal leading to genocide and massive displacement of Native Americans in the nineteenth century. In 2006, Durant went back further in time to explore what Shanna Ketchum-Heap of Birds and James Loewen refer to as the "origin myth": *Scenes from the Pilgrim Story: Myths, Massacres, and Monuments* (2006) was presented at the Massachusetts College of Art. This installation incorporated diorama displays from the recently closed Plymouth Wax Museum to challenge the perceived

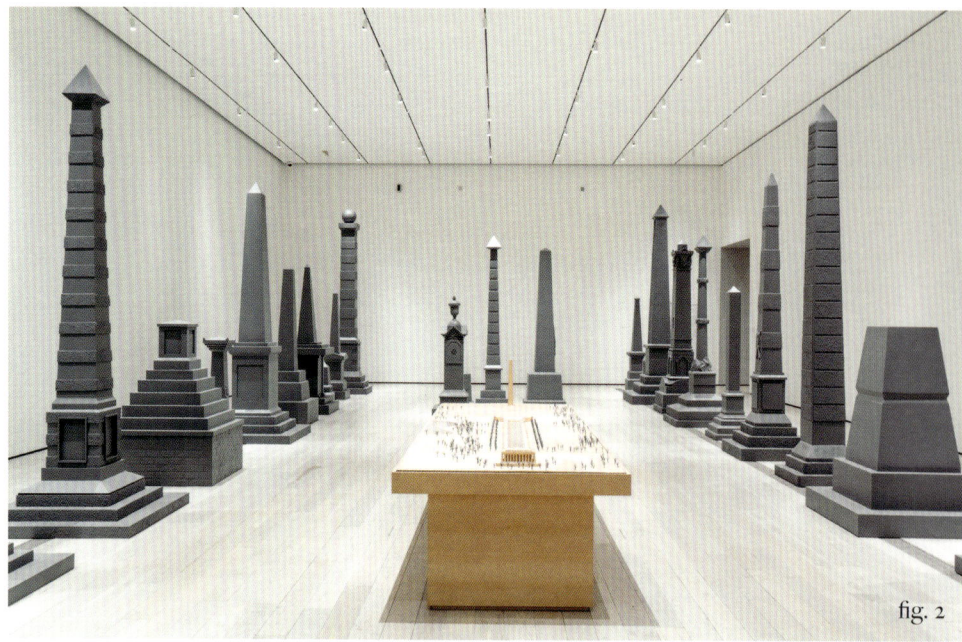

fig. 2

historical narrative of seventeenth-century English colonization. Durant's work turns the saccharine story of friendly cooperation between the English settlers and the resident Wampanoag on its head, proposing that the Pilgrims were engaged in nothing less than genocide (fig. 3).

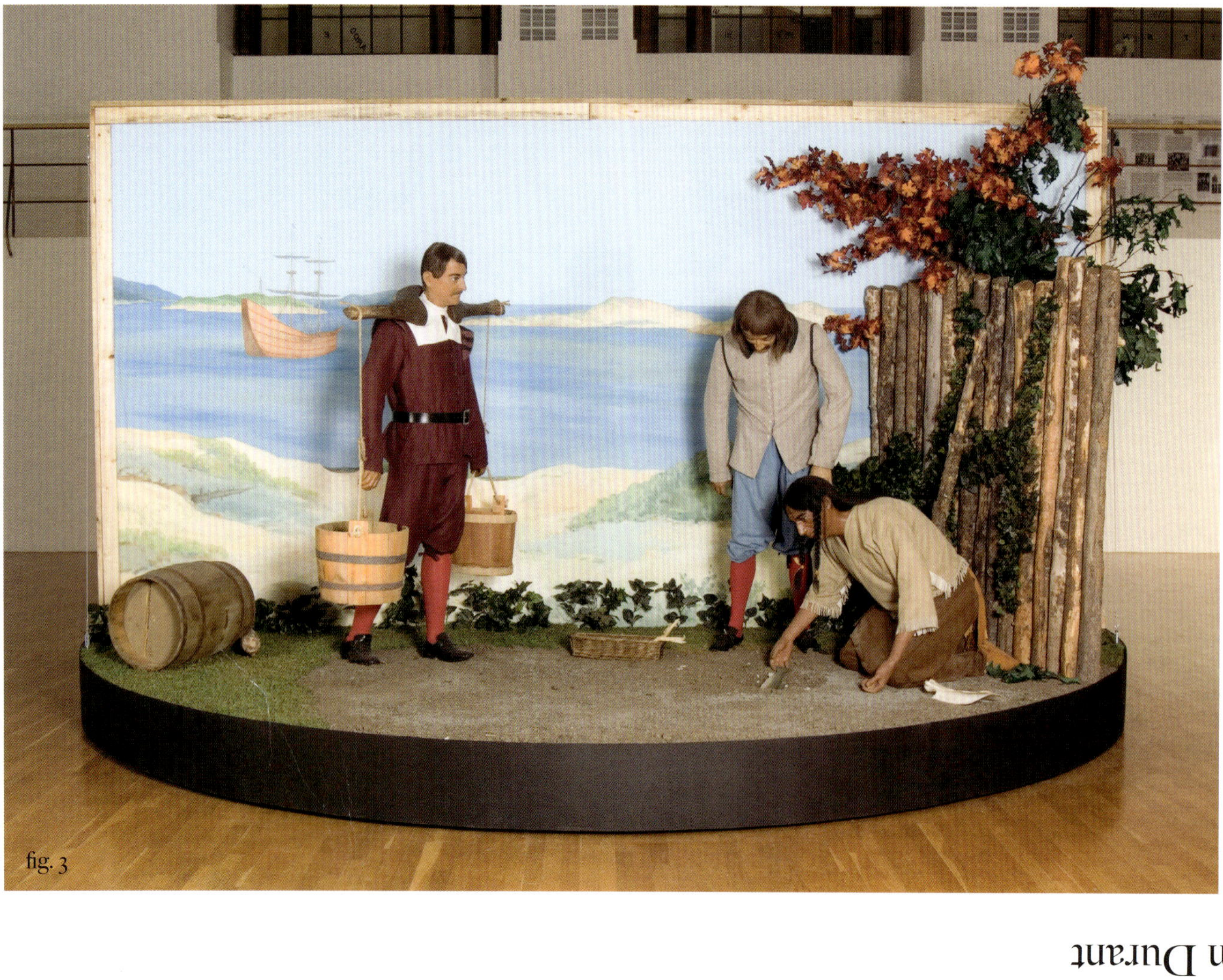

fig. 3

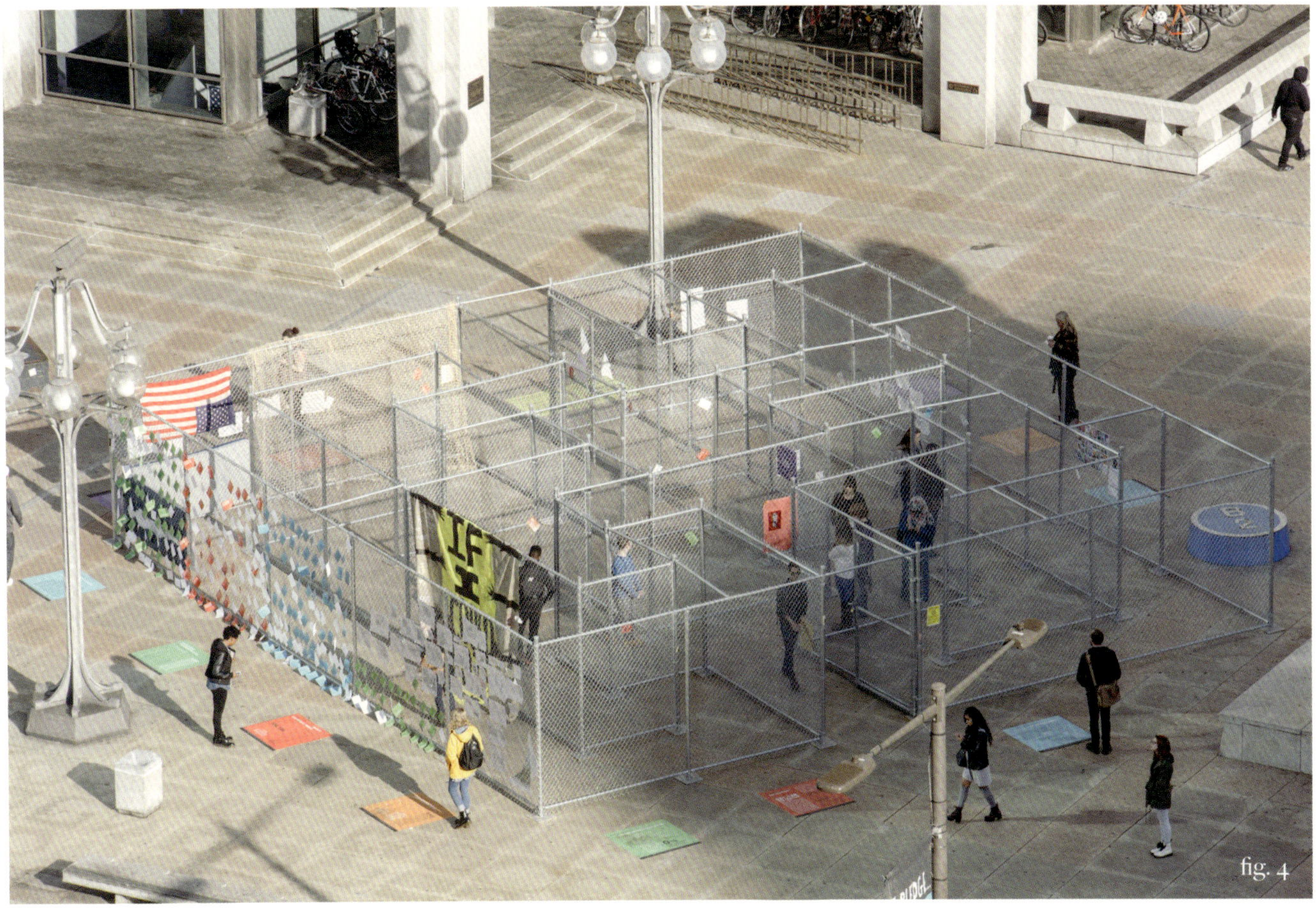

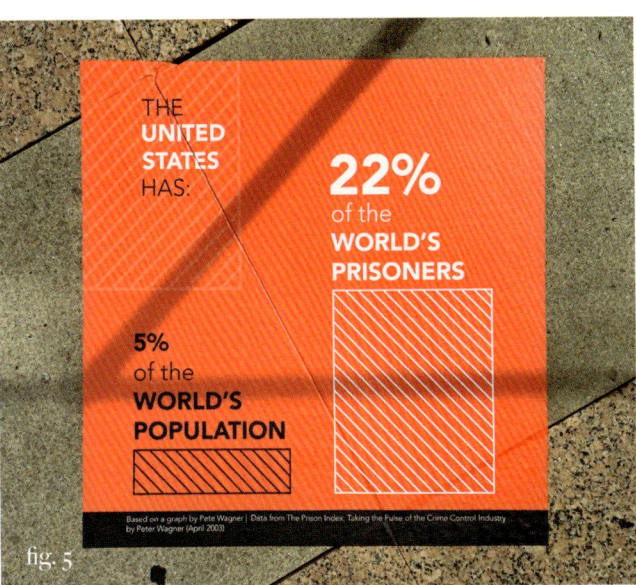

fig. 4

Labyrinth (2015) was the result of a year-long collaboration with a group of artist inmates at Graterford State Prison, the largest maximum-security prison in Pennsylvania, and the Guild, a reentry program for formerly incarcerated individuals and teens on probation (programs both run by the Philadelphia Mural Arts Program) (fig. 4).

What resulted was a 40 × 40 foot chain link fence maze that was placed in the center of Philadelphia across from the iconic City Hall building, surrounded by graphic elements containing troubling statistics related to mass incarceration (fig. 5). In a vital step away from pure representation, the public was invited to hang statements addressing mass incarceration on the maze.

In *The Meeting House*, Durant continues his exploration of these historical omissions and inaccuracies. The project is part of *Art and The Landscape*, a series of public artworks commissioned by The Trustees, a Massachusetts-based conservation group that was founded by the landscape architect Charles Eliot in 1891. As the first and oldest private land trust in the United States, the organization cares for over 116 properties. The Trustees are committed to "protecting special places" such as The Old Manse and to "building creative new programs to engage people." This seemed a perfect context for a project with Sam Durant.

The Old Manse, located in historic Concord, MA, is a National Historic Landmark. The house was built in 1770 by Reverend William Emerson, who was minister of The First Parish in Concord and grandfather to Ralph Waldo Emerson. It has an impressive history from the colonial period through the nineteenth century and is closely associated with the start of the American Revolution. Directly adjacent to the property is the Minuteman National Monument that hosts more than two million visitors a year. Sightseers come to experience the site of the first armed hostilities between British troops and the colonist militia known as the "Minutemen." The battle was immortalized in Ralph Waldo Emerson's poem "Concord Hymn," which contains the phrase "the shot heard round the world."[3] Residents included Rev. Ezra Ripley, Ralph Waldo Emerson, Mary Moody Emerson,

THE UNITED STATES HAS: **22%** of the **WORLD'S PRISONERS**

5% of the **WORLD'S POPULATION**

Based on a graph by Pete Wagner | Data from The Prison Index: Taking the Pulse of the Crime Control Industry by Peter Wagner (April 2003)

fig. 5

and Nathaniel and Sophia Hawthorne, among others. Henry David Thoreau built the vegetable garden and was a handyman, while Louisa May Alcott, her father and sisters, along with many other notable figures of the transcendentalist movement, were regular visitors. Just as important as the colonial and revolutionary history are the literary and intellectual contributions of the nineteenth century that developed in and around The Old Manse. Boston's Poet Laureate Danielle Legros Georges describes American transcendentalism as the "philosophy of the power of the individual, which changed American literature and the imagination."[4] Arguably, America's sense of self, through the conception and popularization of ideas such as self-determination, was born there.

Although Durant had worked extensively with historical and social issues, he had never been granted access to a site of such significance, nor had he worked in a nearly all-white, affluent small town. Furthermore, unlike some of his previous work, *The Meeting House* was not shown inside a museum or gallery but was publicly visible on an unexpected site in the town. From its inception, *The Meeting House* was designed to be highly visible and engage with the community through a series of events, provocative signage, and interventions in the historic home. Durant intended to attract visitors to the site and engender debate, discussion, and solutions to dealing with racism in the US.

The Meeting House is a multifaceted project that functions as a platform for dialogue invoking the legacy of slavery and addressing the institutional and systemic forms of racism facing us today. The work is centered around a pavilion structure installed in the field between The Old Manse and the Minuteman Historic Monument. The architectural structure played host to gatherings and events and also provided space for quiet reflection. The debate and discussion around the issues in the work were structured though a series of public programs entitled "lyceum," a term that was used in the nineteenth century and is closely associated with abolitionism. Additionally visitors would encounter provocative signage surrounding the structure and object-based interventions inside The Old Manse. The project began with community meetings with the local stakeholders, museums, historical homes, and cultural organizations in Concord. The installation and programming were developed in close consultation with the local community and The Trustees staff.

From the beginning Durant was guided by several key historical studies: Henry David Thoreau's *Walden* (1854), Elise Lemire's *Black Walden* (2009), Sandra Harbert Petrulionis' *To Set This World Right: The Antislavery Movement in Thoreau's Concord* (2006), and Lily Geismer's *Don't Blame Us: Suburban Liberals and the Transformation of the Democratic Party* (2014). This research revealed one of the central contradictions in the creation of an independent United States. Claiming that all men are created equal, the Americans were fighting for freedom and liberty, while maintaining the institution of slavery. This sentiment is eloquently spelled out by the English loyalist who composed the epitaph carved on John Jack's grave marker, where it still quietly resides in the Old Hill Burying Ground (fig. 6).

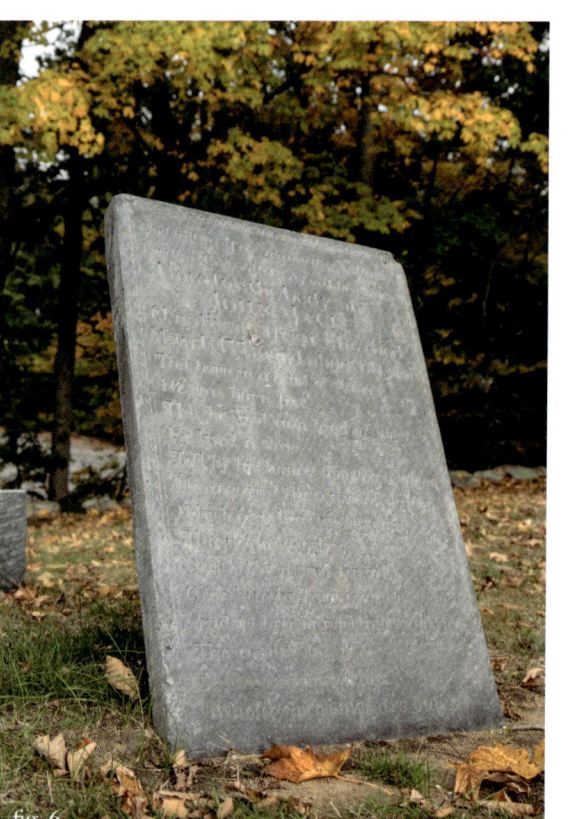

fig. 6

God wills us free, man wills us slaves.
I will as God wills Gods will be done
Here lies the body of JOHN JACK,
A native of Africa who died
March 1773 aged about 60 years
Tho' born in a land of slavery,
He was born free.
Tho' he lived in a land of liberty,
He lived a slave.
Till by his honest tho' stolen labors,
He acquired the source of slavery.
Which gave him his freedom:
Tho' not long before,
Death the grand tyrant,
Gave him his final emancipation,
And set him on a footing with kings,
Tho' a slave to vice.
He practised those virtues
Without which kings are but slaves.

Durant worked with Teddy Cruz and Fonna Forman, celebrated urbanists and political theorists, to develop the design for the pavilion structure. Unlike the hidden history guarded within many historic buildings, the pavilion would be an unenclosed, transparent structure. Engaging the past, but presenting possibilities for a more open future. The pavilion was composed of a dynamic tent-like framework with a bright yellow canopy that spanned a 64-foot-long by 36-foot-wide platform. The stage on which the framework and canopy rested was structured to resemble the four walls of a house, as if it had been thrust open and laid down flat on the ground. This house that formed the foundation of the whole project was based on the homes constructed by the first generation of free Africans in the town of Concord. Many African men and women of this generation lived in Walden Woods, where more than fifty years previously Thoreau had made the name Walden almost synonymous with American identity.

Within this framework Durant curated four lyceum events, free and open to the public, to lay out the parameters of the project. Each lyceum addressed different aspects of racial discrimination.

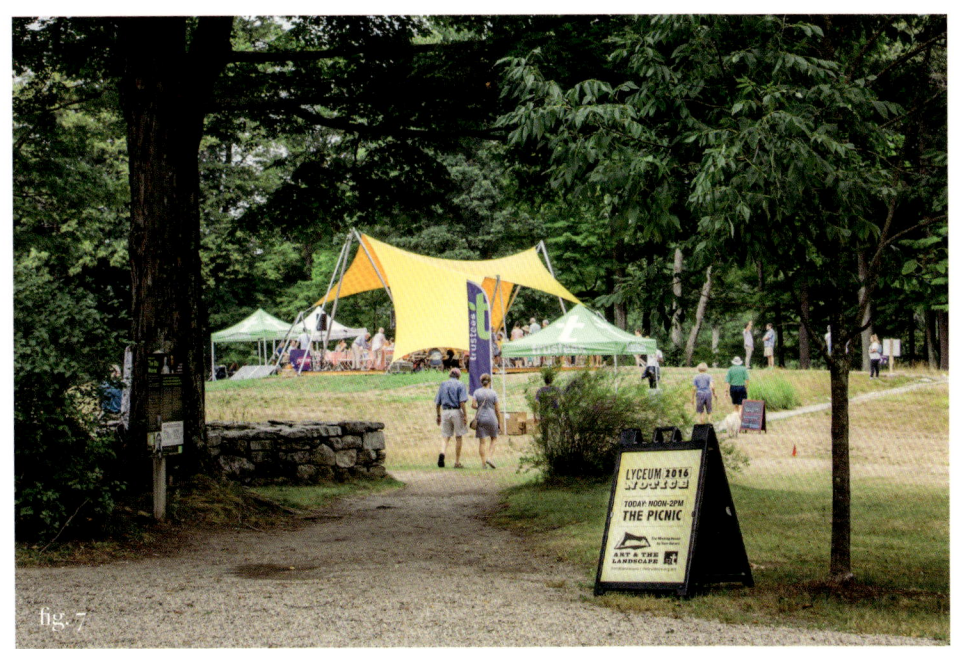

fig. 7

Phillips brought together four remarkable leaders who are already succeeding in creating a more just, equitable, and peaceful world. Former Boston Assistant District Attorney Adam Foss runs a national training program to reduce racial bias in the prosecutors' office and mentors at-risk youth. Gilead Sher, an Israeli negotiator involved in the Camp David Summit and the Oslo Accords, talked of the importance of resilience in the struggle to resolve ongoing conflicts. Barbara Lewis heads the Trotter Institute for the Study of Black History and Culture at UMass Boston, and her work has bridged the gap between community and campus through programs promoting urban cultural history. Former human resources and diversity officer for major private and public sector organizations like Harvard University, Staples, and Bank of Boston, Penny Outlaw now runs the Royall House and Slave Quarters, educating tourists and students about the inextricable bond between slavery and wealth in New England. The conversation revealed the complexities of dealing with racial discrimination as well as productive ways of addressing these issues.

Thoreau writes about the "previous inhabitants" of the Walden Woods, referring to the emancipated Africans who inhabited the area around Walden Pond.[5] In *Black Walden*, Elise Lemire reveals that newly free African men and women were allowed to squat around Walden Pond and struggled to survive in the largely infertile land available to them.[6] Africans labored to obtain proper nutrition in the regions of land allotted to them in colonial times—a situation that is mirrored in the food deserts that currently prevail in many inner city neighborhoods. *Lyceum I—The Picnic* consisted of a feast intended to bring communities together to celebrate African American food culture (fig. 7). Fulani Hayes, a retired nurse turned food activist, led the discussion about her work in Boston teaching children organic gardening, nutrition, and healthy cooking.

Transcendentalism is commonly recognized as a literary movement, and one that played a major role in creating American identity. While someone like Frederick Douglass could easily be included, transcendentalism is a movement that excluded African American writers and intellectuals. For *Lyceum II—Poetry Reading*, Durant commissioned four leading African American poets to respond to the site and its history. After Tisa Bryant, Robin Coste Lewis, Danielle Legros Georges, and Kevin Young read their powerful and moving new works, the audience engaged in a lively discussion. In one response to questions, Young pointed out the shortcomings of enlightenment, proposing instead that we might need to "endarken" our history.

Tim Phillips of Beyond Conflict was invited to create *Lyceum III —A New Framework for Dialogue*.

Lyceum IV—New England Town Hall Meeting took place at the First Parish Church, where William Emerson and Ezra Ripley served as ministers in the late eighteenth and early nineteenth centuries. Based on the format of a town meeting, three articles were drafted and presented in order, structured as an open discussion. Mary Jane Jacob, a pioneer of socially engaged art, led the meeting and responded to people's remarks and questions (fig. 8).

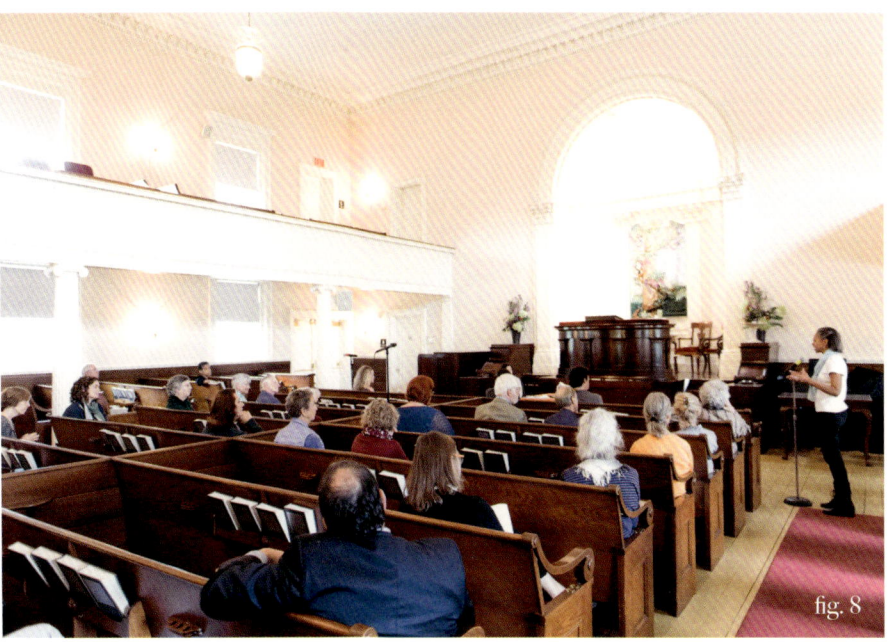

fig. 8

While the lyceums served as discussion platforms, five signs surrounding the pavilion structure created some controversy in the town (fig. 9). Provoking discomfort was an alternative to the presentation of facts and reasoning, the latter, which—perhaps surprisingly—can be ineffective in engendering attitude or behavior changes. The sign that inspired the most debate read:

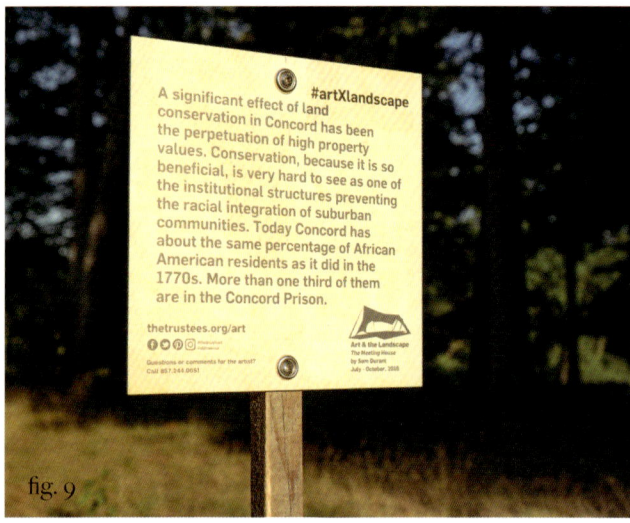

fig. 9

The statement draws attention to an uncomfortable consequence of well-intended policies and practices that limit prosperity for African Americans. Durant was looking into the generational transfer of wealth through the inheritance of property. Historically and even today, general housing and lending discrimination have prevented African Americans from purchasing homes and bequeathing them to their heirs. The Federal Reserve Bank of Boston released a study in 2015 finding that the median net worth of whites in Boston is $247,000, while the median net worth of African Americans is $8.[7] Homeownership is the single greatest factor in net worth. The current inequality that manifests itself across the nation in crime, poverty, education, and mass incarceration is directly related to discriminatory lending policies, redlining, and selective law enforcement. Whilst being provocative and creating a zone of discomfort, *The Meeting House* was not intended to shame individuals but to acknowledge the past and its effect in present-day society.

Another component of *The Meeting House* took place inside The Old Manse. Inspired by artist Fred Wilson's *Mining the Museum* (1992), Durant inserted new objects and elements into the house. This intervention created a new narrative inside the historic national landmark. Objects included reproductions of land deeds for homes owned by emancipated Africans in the early nineteenth century and broadside notices from the 1850s warning Africans about slave catchers and police, one from the Concord Anti-Slavery Society, and one from a women's organization dedicated to abolishing slavery (fig. 10).

Durant also inserted a reproduction of a Phillis Wheatley manuscript in the second-floor-study where Ralph Waldo Emerson wrote his first book *Nature* in 1835 and Nathaniel Hawthorne wrote *Mosses from an Old Manse* in 1842. In a simple gesture, Durant relates the work of two literary titans recognized as seminal figures in American thought and literature with the work of Wheatley, an enslaved woman, who in 1773 was the first African to publish a book of poetry in English.[8]

The experience of creating *The Meeting House* led Durant to continue exploring the region's history and to develop work for the exhibition *Build Therefore Your Own World* at Blum & Poe gallery in Los Angeles. The title is a fragment sourced from Ralph Waldo Emerson; the full quotation is used in the titling of the major work for the exhibition. In the two months between the dismantling of *The Meeting House* in Concord, MA, and the opening of the exhibition in Los Angeles, sections of the pavilion were shipped west to California. These panels served as material to form the centerpiece, *"Every spirit builds itself a house, and beyond its house a world...Build therefore your own world"* (2017). The pavilion flooring that had simulated the walls of the first homes of free Africans was erected to conjure a home within the gallery. Now functioning as walls, the floorboards that supported the lyceum events were used like lined sheets of paper on which to render a selection of poems composed by Bryant, Coste Lewis, Young, and Legros Georges for the second lyceum. The sculpture becomes a house of language, re-inhabited by poetry and spirit, and pointing toward the freedom to build oneself a world, a possibility that has been largely denied to African Americans.

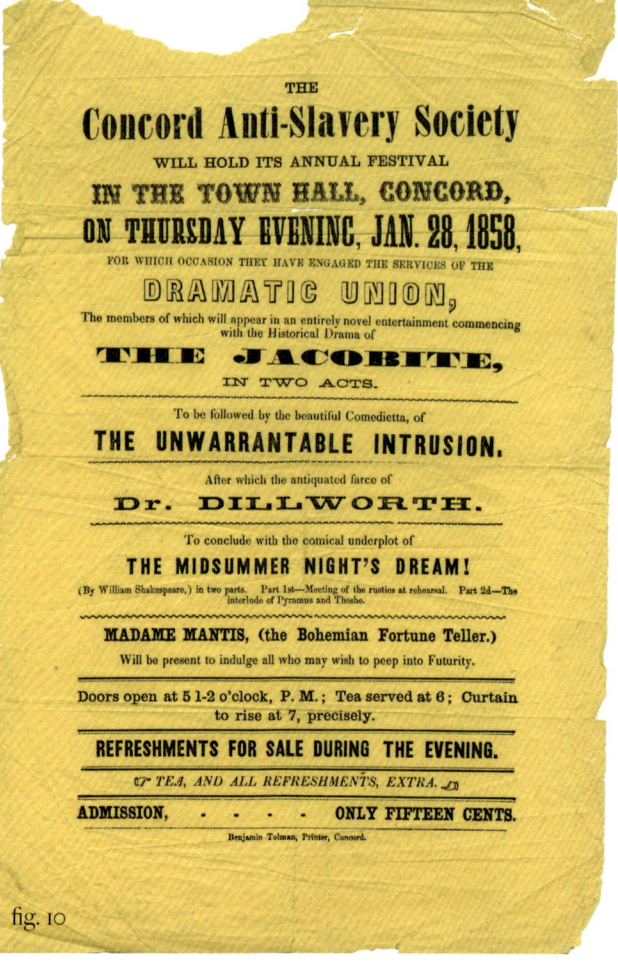

fig. 10

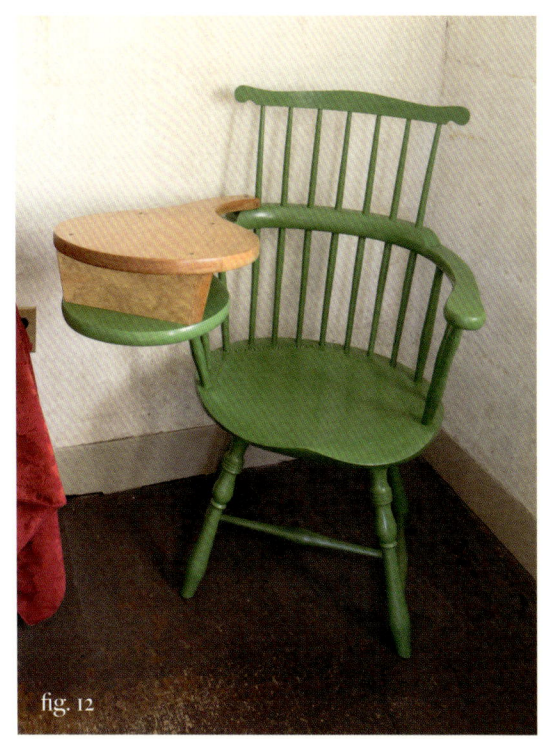

fig. 11

fig. 12

Durant describes the exhibition as representing the "inseparability of African American cultural pioneers from the canonical transcendentalists and American identity itself."[9] He created new works using representations of a selection of historical artifacts and combined them to make a statement about the hybrid nature of culture and race. *Transcendental* (*Wheatley's Desk, Emerson's Chair*) (2016) is a composite of the desks of two iconic literary figures: Phillis Wheatley (fig. 11) and Ralph Waldo Emerson (fig. 12). Like the intervention in Hawthorne and Emerson's study in The Old Manse, this is another reminder of the African poet whose work preceded both men by more than half a century.

Erasure, Appearance (*Garrison's Walking Stick, Thoreau's Pencil*) (2016) is composed of reproductions of Jack Garrison's walking stick and a pencil from Thoreau's father's factory. In the 1800s the town of Concord awarded Jack Garrison, a self-emancipated slave from New Jersey, a walking stick on his birthday. This work speaks to the fluidity of history; how individuals and objects can be used as symbols to generate a narrative favoring those in power. Lemire points out that abolitionists used the only known image of Garrison as a symbol of the town's commitment to freedom in order to obscure Concord's history of slavery and discrimination.[10]

Fieldstones (after Robin Coste Lewis' Erasures) (2016) displays bronze casts of fieldstones collected by the artist in Massachusetts, inspired by Coste Lewis' poem "Inhabitants and Visitors" (fig. 13). The poem was composed using a technique known as erasure where sections of work by another author are omitted, in this case from Thoreau's *Walden*. In his work Durant asks the viewer to "fill in the blanks" with associations to the term "fieldstone." Fieldstone was

and is a common building material in New England. It is resonant with meaning in the context of seventeenth and eighteenth century slavery—fieldstones, house stones, foundation stones. Martin Luther King wrote about slavery in New England:

> In fact, this ghastly blood traffic was so immense and its profits were so stupendous that the economies of several European nations owed their growth and prosperity to it and New England rested heavily on it for its development. [Charles A.] Beard declared it was fair to say of whole towns in New England and Great Britain: 'The stones of your houses are cemented with the blood of African slaves.'[11]

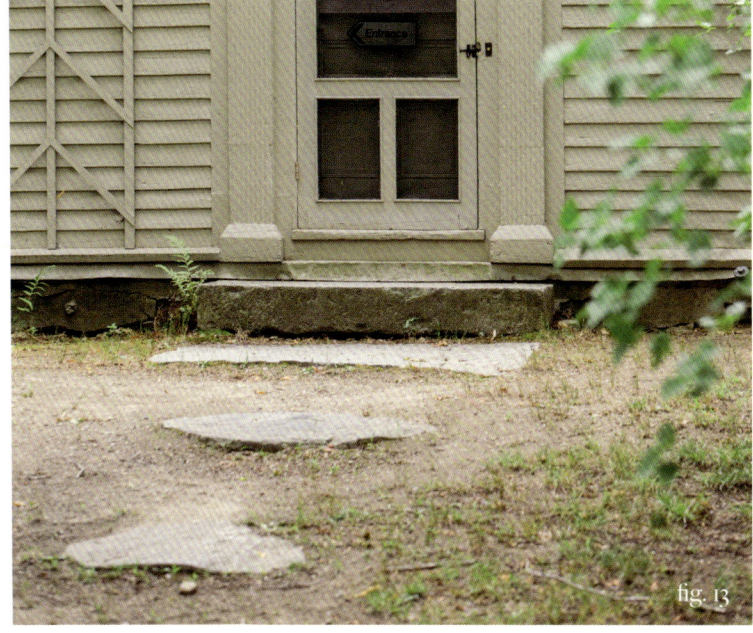

fig. 13

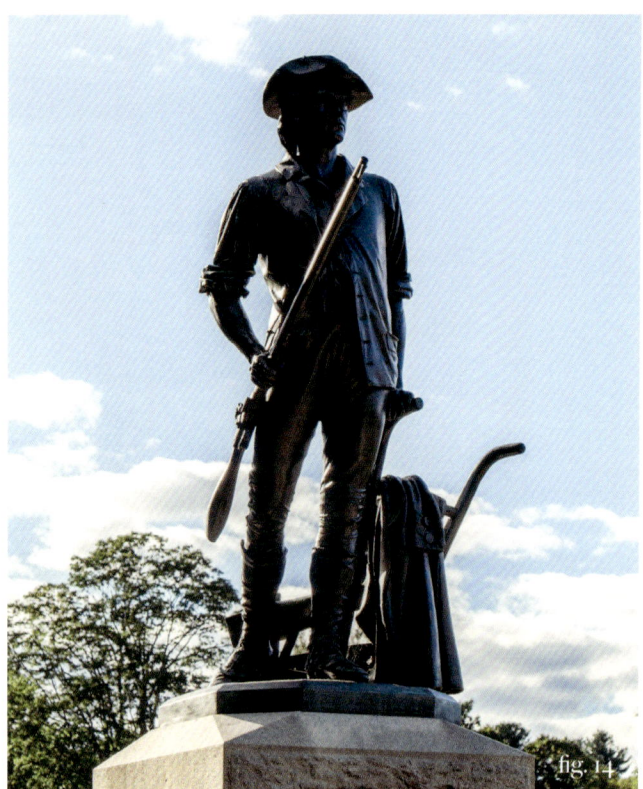

fig. 14

The process of erasing words to create a poem is similar to the process of omitting individuals and their contributions to history. The narrative is created by removing what is inconvenient or undesired, allowing white supremacy to remain invisible and the status quo for white America. Durant's sign (fig. 15) responds to Daniel Chester French's famous *Minute Man* statue (fig. 14) with a suggestion paraphrasing Lemire's conclusion to *Black Walden*:

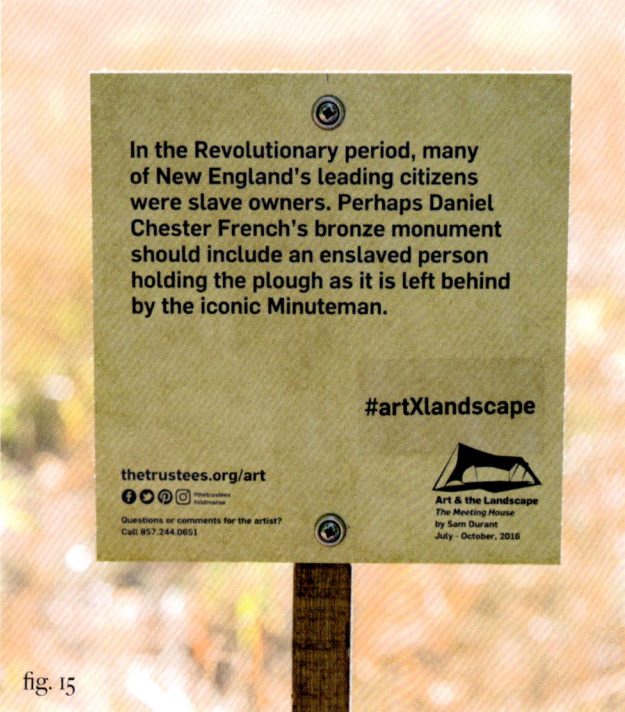

In the Revolutionary period, many of New England's leading citizens were slave owners. Perhaps Daniel Chester French's bronze monument should include an enslaved person holding the plough as it is left behind by the iconic Minuteman.

#artXlandscape

thetrustees.org/art

Art & the Landscape
The Meeting House
by Sam Durant
July - October, 2016

Questions or comments for the artist?
Call 857.244.0651

fig. 15

At a moment when it is very easy to live in an information bubble, surrounded by like-minded individuals with a similar life experience and opinions, *The Meeting House* compels us to look inside ourselves, pulling us away from our daily practice of social media and hyper-connectivity. Durant challenges viewers to reconsider prevailing forms of racism that are easy for white people to ignore. *The Meeting House* was a temporary intervention intended to stimulate dialogue about race. An artwork such as this can reflect a community's tolerance for divergent ideas, new social norms and competing narratives. It provides new perspectives and enables communication, questioning preconceived notions about race and the role of art as a vehicle to address such intractable issues.

The consequences of discrimination for those who have not personally experienced them can be abstract and overwhelming. Durant's work in Concord was inspired by the town's rich history, not by the residents' socioeconomic status and race. However, the resulting conversations and reactions to *The Meeting House*, positive and negative, illuminated the importance of taking this dialogue to predominantly white suburbs where the consequences of racial discrimination are easily ignored. As Durant pointed out, "Race is actually an issue for whites. We are the ones that created it and yet don't see it. We can no longer remain unaware."[12] The experience in Concord revealed the critical importance of whites across the nation engaging in meaningful exchange about racial discrimination. The artist Rick Lowe stated that in the twentieth century Blacks led the struggle for racial equality.[13] In the twenty-first century, it's time for whites to step up, it's your turn!

1   Sam Durant, in discussion with the author, September 2016.

2   Shanna Ketchum-Heap of Birds, "On Legitimizing the Body Politic: America's Founding Myth Reconsidered," *Sam Durant: Scenes from the Pilgrim Story: Myths, Massacres, and Monuments* (Boston, MA: Stephen D. Paine Gallery and Massachusetts College of Art, 2007).

3   Ralph Waldo Emerson, "Concord Hymn," *Yale Book of American Verse*, ed. Thomas Raynesford Lounsbury (New Haven: Yale University Press, 1912).

4   Danielle Legros Georges, "Fall into the Arts Segment 2," City Line broadcast, WCVB On Demand, video, 08:54, September 4, 2016, http://www.wcvb.com/article/sunday-september-4-2016-fall-into-art/8247293.

5   Henry David Thoreau, *Walden: Or, Life in the Woods*, rev. ed. (New York: Dover Publications, 1995).

6   Elise Lemire, *Black Walden: Slavery and Its Aftermath in Concord, Massachusetts* (Philadelphia: University of Pennsylvania Press, 2009).

7   Ana Patricia Muñoz, et al., eds., *The Color of Wealth in Boston*, report for the Federal Reserve Bank of Boston (Durham, NC: The New School and Duke University, 2015).

8   Henry Louis Gates Jr., *The Trials of Phillis Wheatley: America's First Black Poet and Her Encounters with the Founding Fathers* (New York: Basic Civitas Books, 2003).

9   Sam Durant, *Build Therefore Your Own World* exhibition proposal to Blum & Poe, 2016.

10 Lemire, *Black Walden*, 171–73.

11 Martin Luther King, *Where Do We Go From Here: Chaos or Community?*, (Boston, MA: Beacon Press, 1968), 75.

12 Sam Durant, in discussion with the author, October 2016.

13 Rick Lowe, "The Art of Inclusion: Making the Invisible Visible", keynote panel moderated by the author, conference, MIT Media Lab, October 28–29, 2016.

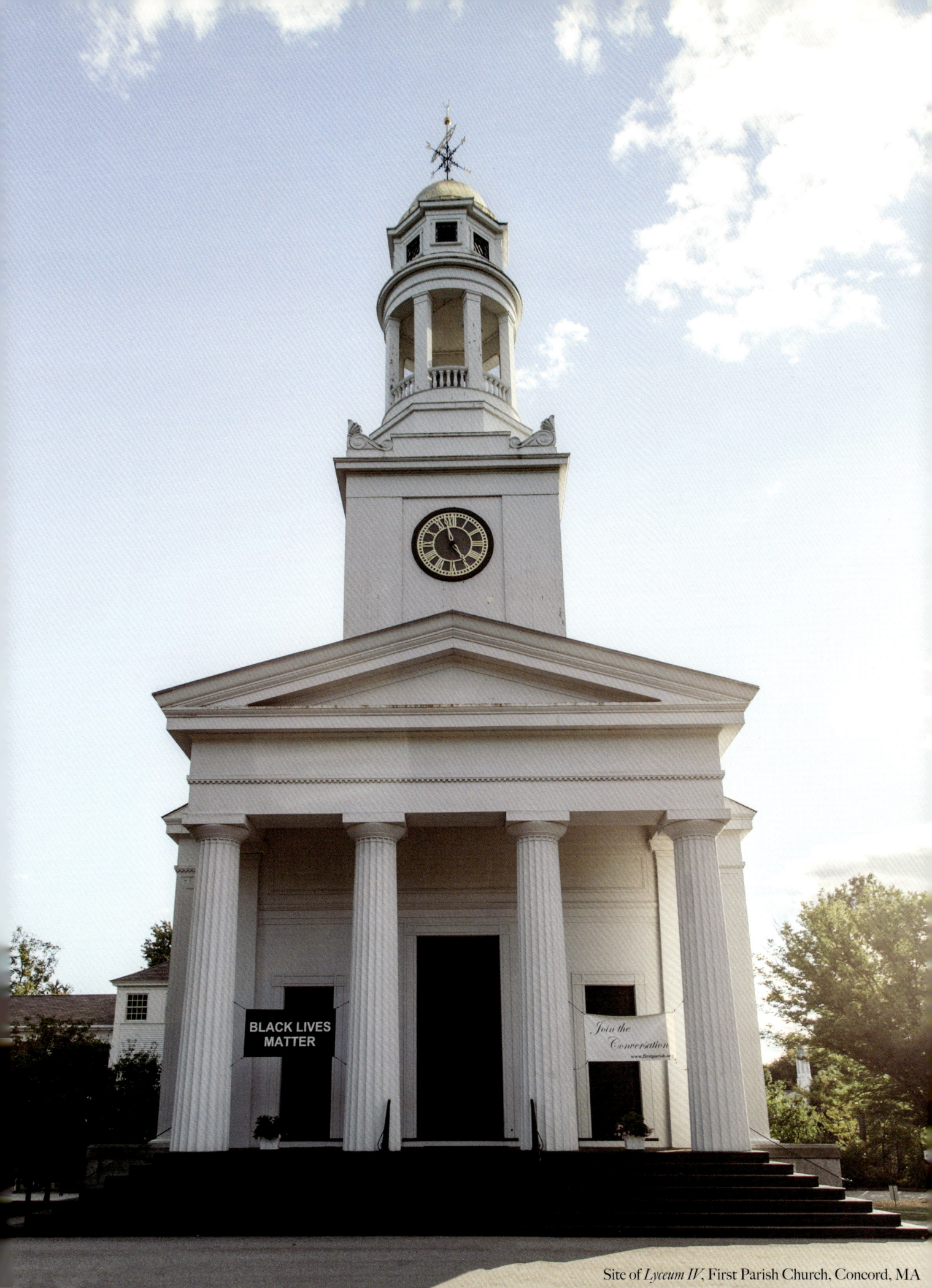

Site of *Lyceum IV*, First Parish Church, Concord, MA

Making the Invisible Visible

Art and Context as an Instrument of Social Change

Tim Phillips

Tim Phillips

I have spent the last twenty-five years working with leaders around the world who have struggled to move their countries from dictatorship to democracy and from conflict to peace. Using the shared human experience approach, which I developed in the early 1990s, my organization, Beyond Conflict, brings together leaders struggling with profound social and political change with those who previously led transitions in other countries. Our belief is that people can learn from the experience of others, and seeing that others have overcome similar, once-intractable problems provides them with the courage and capacity to lead positive change in their own countries and communities.

Using this approach, we have supported leaders in Central and Eastern Europe and the former Soviet Union as they confronted the legacy of seventy years of Communist rule and repression; helped South Africans to create their Truth and Reconciliation Commission in the painful aftermath of apartheid; encouraged leaders in Northern Ireland to imagine the possibility of peace after decades of division and violence; and worked to promote reconciliation in the aftermath of war in Central America and the Balkans. Most recently, we helped set the conditions for the breakthrough between Cuba and the United States after six decades of polarization, and we continue to promote reconciliation between both countries and to work with Cuban Americans seeking to find a new way forward in order to heal their community after decades of exile and suffering.

The shared human experience approach has proven to be a powerful and transformative model for change because it is founded on the recognition that individuals—no matter where they live, no matter their race, ethnicity, religion, or gender—can learn from the experience of others who have struggled to overcome deep-seated fear and division, and through the example of those others can develop their own capacity to lead positive change.

Through my work, I have come to recognize that there are fundamental drivers of conflict and reconciliation that exist at the national, international, and personal levels. Drivers that are not defined by culture, ethnicity, or geography, but are instead driven by one's universal human need to be acknowledged, understood, and validated as one sees oneself. My experience shows that all conflict—whether at the national or personal level—is driven by exclusion, by the experience of being marginalized and ignored, and by the failure to recognize adequately and acknowledge the identity of others. Individuals and communities have a longing and a need to be included, and to be agents of their own destinies. In fact, neuroscientists using brain-imaging technology have found that the brain registers social rejection the same way that it registers physical pain. The region of the brain that processes trauma cannot fully differentiate between emotional and physical trauma, and scientists tell us that we cannot fully access our capacity for rational thought until we feel that our identities are genuinely understood and valued by others.

When I look at the profound challenges we face in the United States concerning race, inclusion, and the growing divide between different communities throughout the country, I see the same dynamics at play that I have seen around the world. This comes as no surprise. Human brains are wired the same way, no matter where their possessors live or what they do. Our survival as a species has depended on feeling safe, secure, and empowered to make decisions about our own futures as *we* envision them. These deep and basic human needs are the root of conflict and reconciliation, whether on the global stage or in our communities and families. Efforts to achieve peace in Northern Ireland and to end apartheid peacefully in South Africa succeeded only when all parties, even the smallest and most marginalized, were brought to a table where the dominant parties did not impose their will, and when communities felt they had agency over their own future—in short, when they felt acknowledged, valued, and safe.

When one looks at the tensions in the world today, one witnesses an urgent and growing demand from individuals and communities to be heard and recognized as fully human, that is, seeking to be treated with dignity, respect, and as equal members of a shared community. The most powerful and transcendent lessons we can learn from other nations that have experienced profound change is that peace and reconciliation became truly possible only when all groups in a given country were included in every important decision about their future. As the often-quoted Northern Irish slogan goes, "nothing about us, without us."

Behavioral science overwhelmingly confirms that there is a biological basis for much of our behavior—particularly for our powerful need to be included, acknowledged, and seen as we see ourselves. Research on sacred values—those values we hold that are above compromise and that are key to our identity and sense of place in the world, such as the protection of our children, the principles of our religion, or family honor—are processed in different regions of the brain than more utilitarian or businesslike thoughts. The research shows that when we are asked to compromise our sacred values, we hold on to them more deeply and respond with anger and aggression. It is only when our sacred values are recognized by others that we begin to listen. When we don't feel under threat, when our core identities are acknowledged as we define them, then we are able to think rationally and begin the process of opening our minds to others with views fundamentally different than our own.

With these powerful insights, gleaned from experience and confirmed by science, it is clear, and powerfully so, that artists, particularly visual artists, have a vital and unique role to play in helping individuals to navigate these powerful realities. Art, at its best, fundamentally challenges the way that we see the world and confronts us with realities that beg us to look deeper at what we believe to be true. Artists have the power to reveal truths when words alone are not enough to make others hear and see. Art can force the viewer to consider other realities and other narratives; to recognize connections where other means fail to do so.

But to stop at revealing certain truths without providing context would be a disservice to the pursuit of truth. For what behavioral science clearly demonstrates and experience confirms is that empathy—the biological capacity of members of our species to place themselves in the minds of another and access a part of that other's truth—is dependent on context and proximity. The searing and disturbing image of the young Syrian boy,

Alan Kurdi, who drowned as his family sought refuge in Europe and washed up on the beach in Turkey, did more to connect the world to the brutality of war in Syria then the thousands of images of civilians fleeing bombed-out Aleppo and the countless other moments of suffering and death that were reported. The unique power of that truth came from the reality that we all could imagine that child belonging to us. He was dressed in shorts and sneakers, and his young, lifeless body was washed up on a beach that looked like a beach on which we may have once vacationed. Seeing that young boy in a context that our minds could access so directly and unconsciously resulted in more awareness and attention to the plight of Syrian refugees than all the news stories and photos that documented the many horrors of the war in Syria.

voice, about making the invisible visible and showing us truths about the human experience that we might not otherwise see. Sam Durant did that powerfully at The Old Manse in Concord, Massachusetts. The lyceum he created, literally on one of the most sacred grounds in American history, powerfully contextualized narratives we knew about the first battle of the American Revolution alongside lesser-known narratives about the history of slavery and the treatment of African Americans, from the founding of the colony to the present day. Durant placed unknown and often uncomfortable narratives about African American life in Concord over three centuries in the context of a space that is about liberty, freedom, and human dignity. The viewer wasn't shouted down or humiliated. The viewer was presented with deep

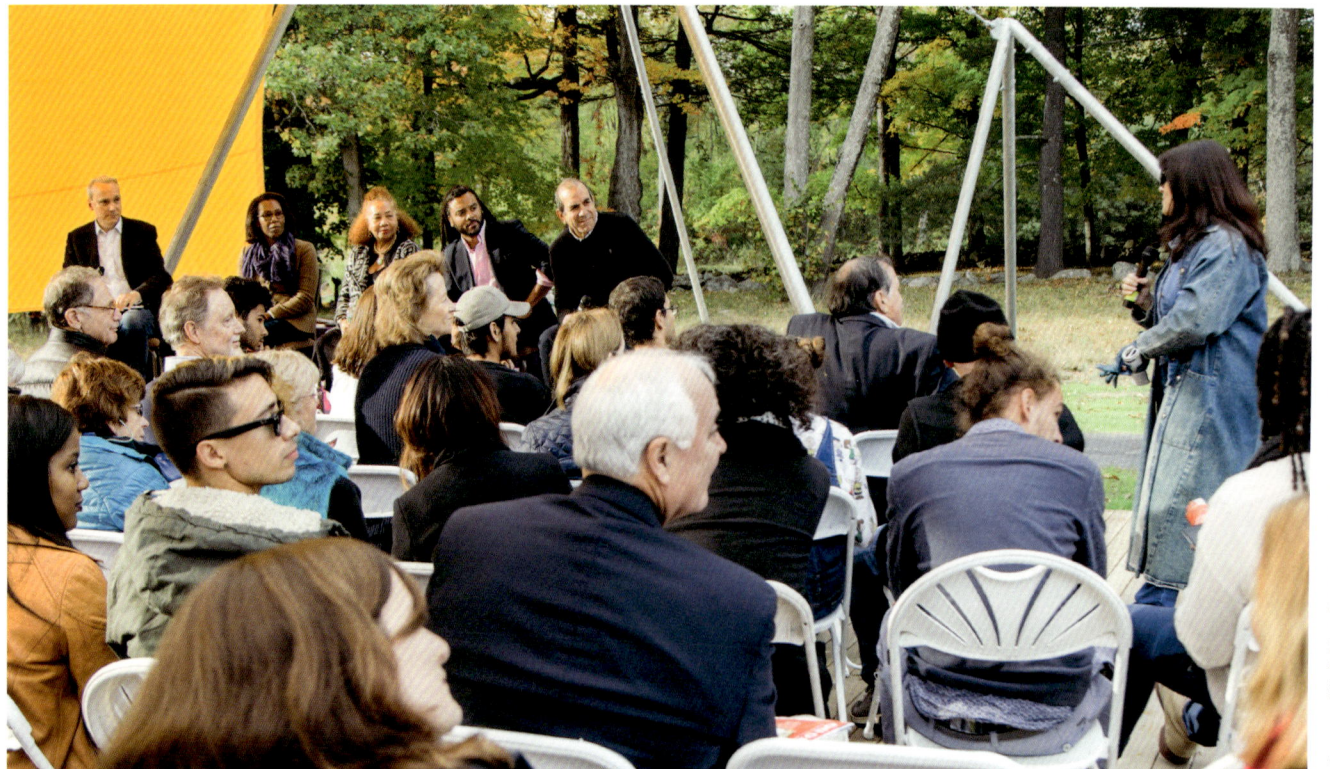

Lyceum III: A New Framework for Dialogue, with (from left, on stage facing the audience): Tim Phillips, Penny Outlaw, Barbara Lewis, Adam Foss, and Gilead Sher.

At this troubling and uncertain time, when social divides are deepening and trust is declining, we must find ways to connect. Artists must not only reflect painful and necessary truths, but they must strive to present them in contexts that allow us to see something about ourselves and to see our own lived experience in others. There is so much that divides us simply by being human. We differ by our social, ethnic, cultural, religious, racial, and political identities. But we are also united by shared values and, most profoundly, by the shared need to feel understood and acknowledged, to feel respected and to have impact on our worlds.

This context, this ability to give meaning, to give voice to others, to empathize with those profoundly different from them, is what leaders from South Africa and Northern Ireland learned to navigate as they sought to end war and repression and reconcile their deeply divided nations. It is what great artists have always been able to do on the personal level. Art is about giving

and painful truths in a setting that was about *liberty*, about farmers who wanted to define for themselves what community and inclusion looked like. By providing context and challenging the visitor with other truths, other narratives, Durant offered the visitor the tools to think, to question and to engage. Visitors to that site may not remember everything that was said in the lyceums, but they won't forget that in that space they learned something about others that they won't easily forget.

Conflict and reconciliation within the United States are no different from conflict and reconciliation around the world—and our challenge of navigating increasingly complex subjective truths is equally profound. We must begin to think deeply about the lived realities of those different from us. This begins with acknowledging our shared humanity, our common need to be heard, understood, and included in fundamental decisions that shape our future; and it begins by inviting those curious enough to explore what is across that threshold—however we define it.

Sam Durant

Sam Durant

The Meeting House

The Old Manse, Concord, Massachusetts
August 13–October 31, 2016

18

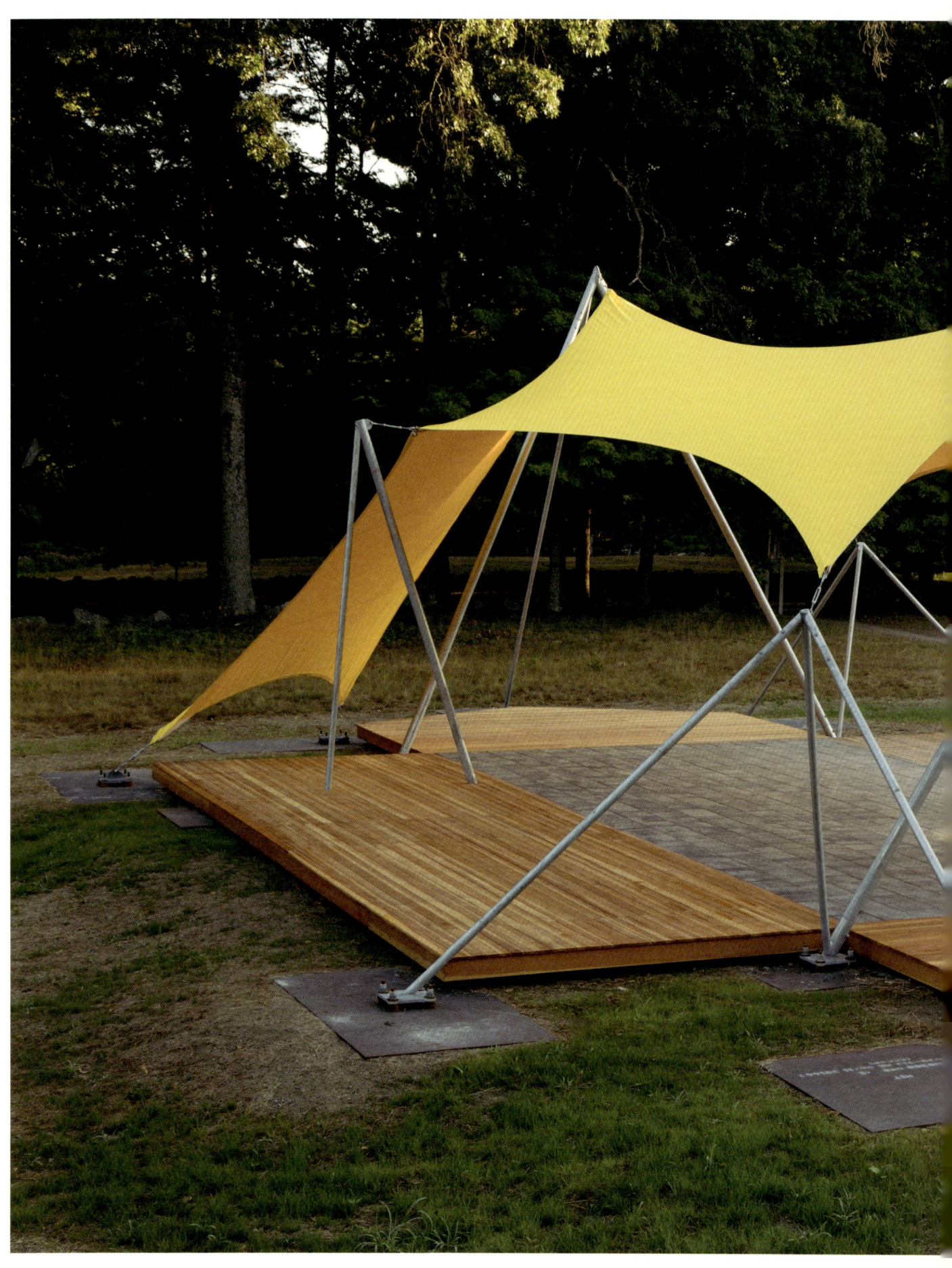

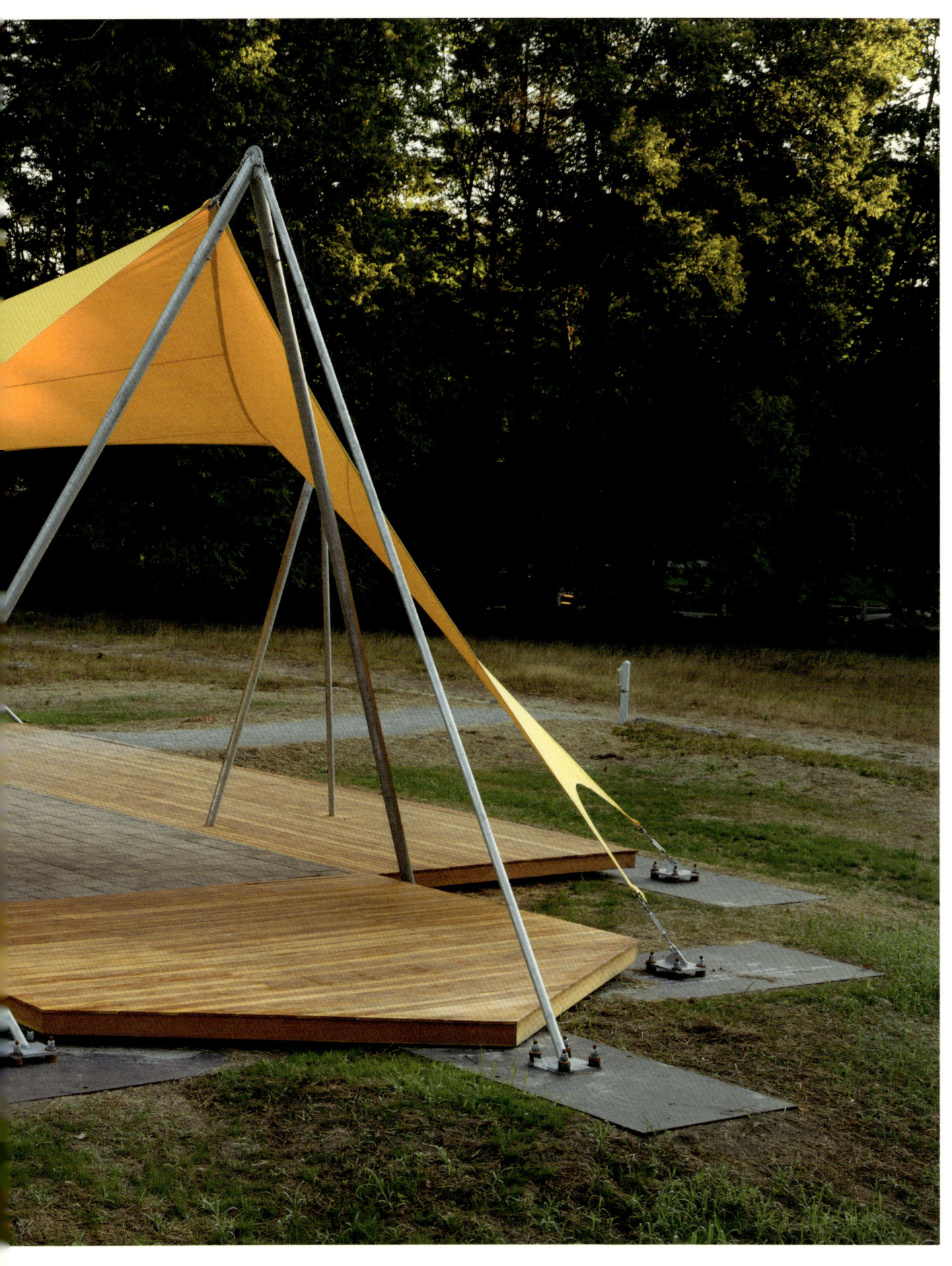

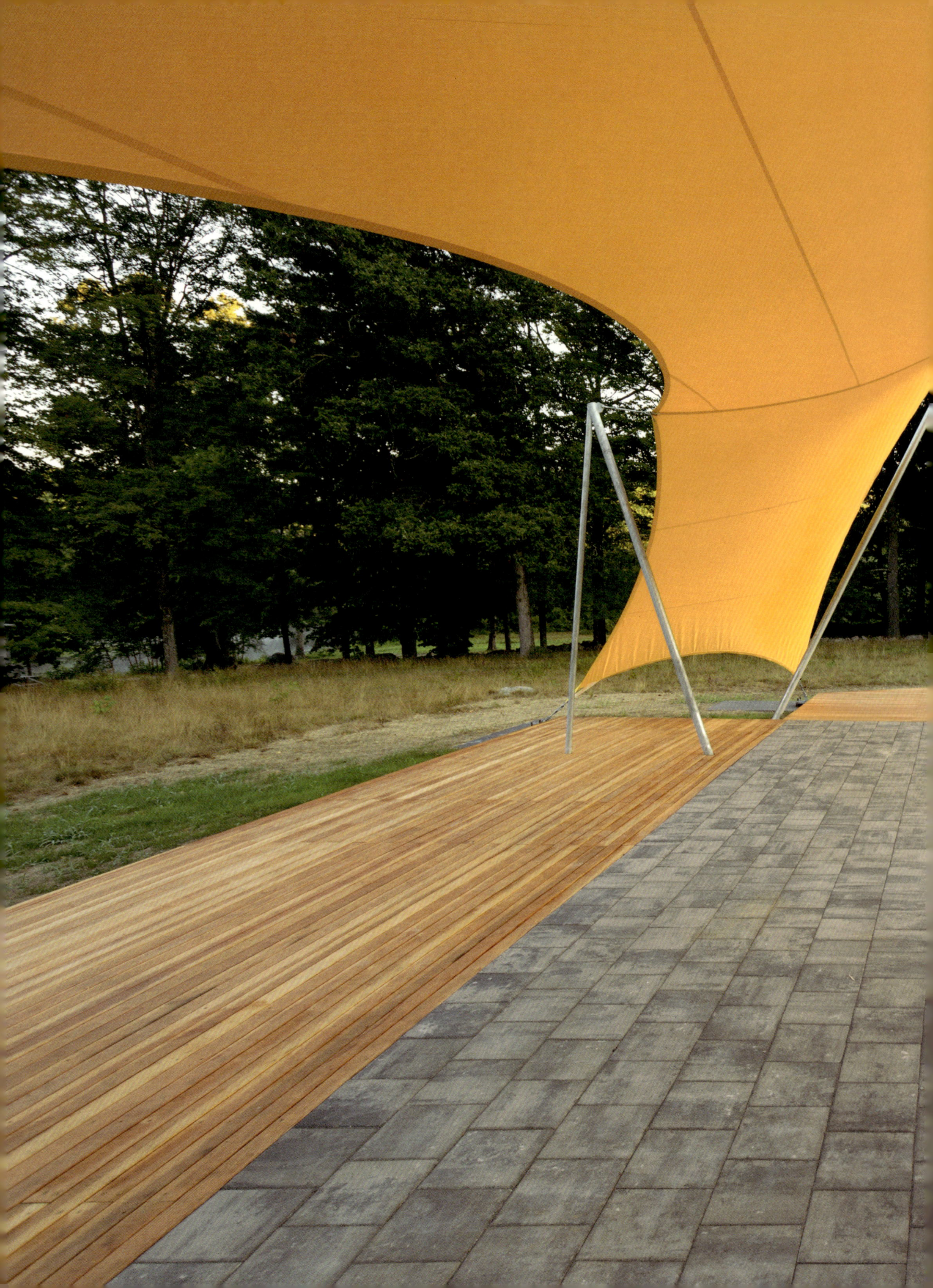

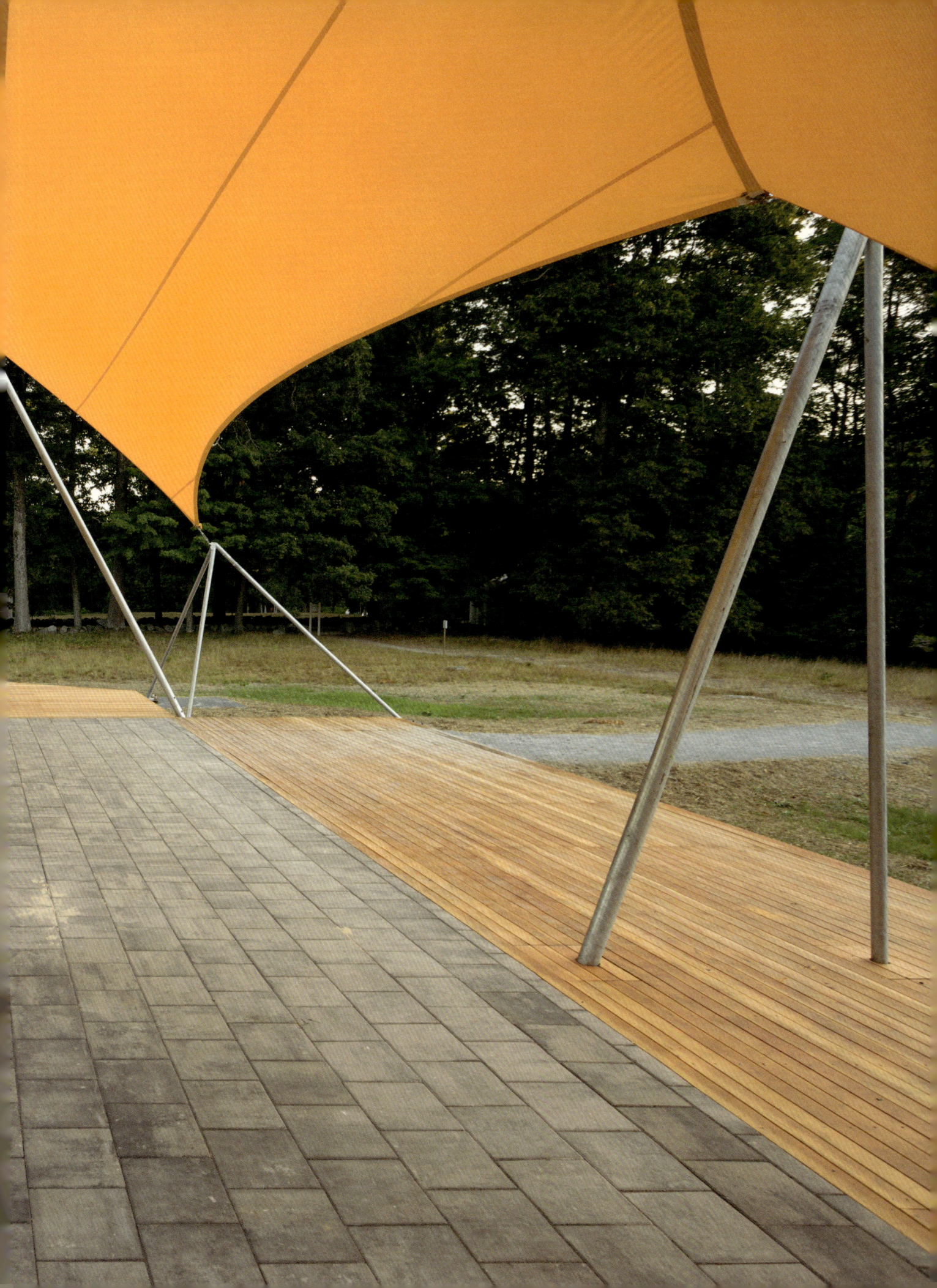

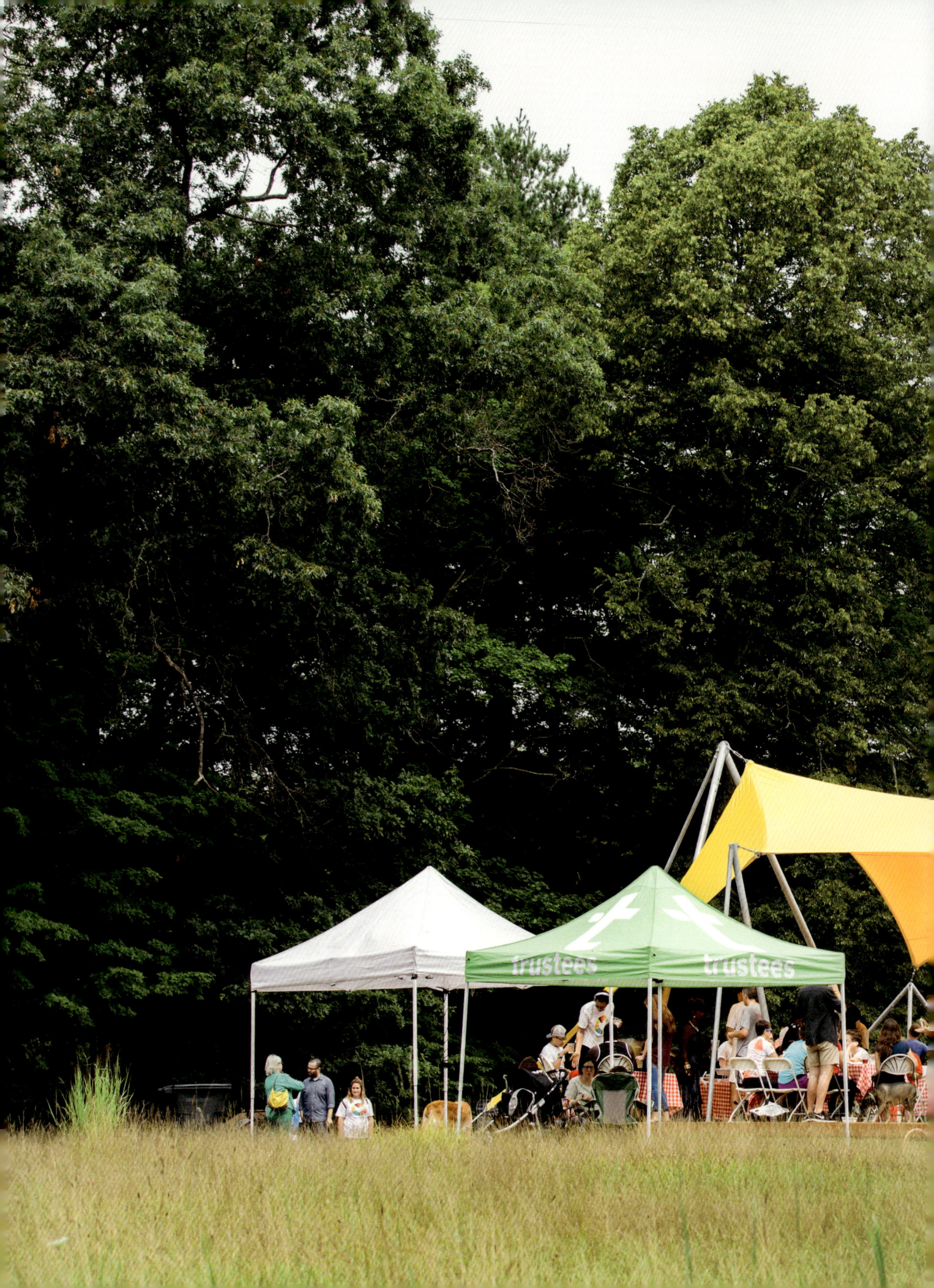

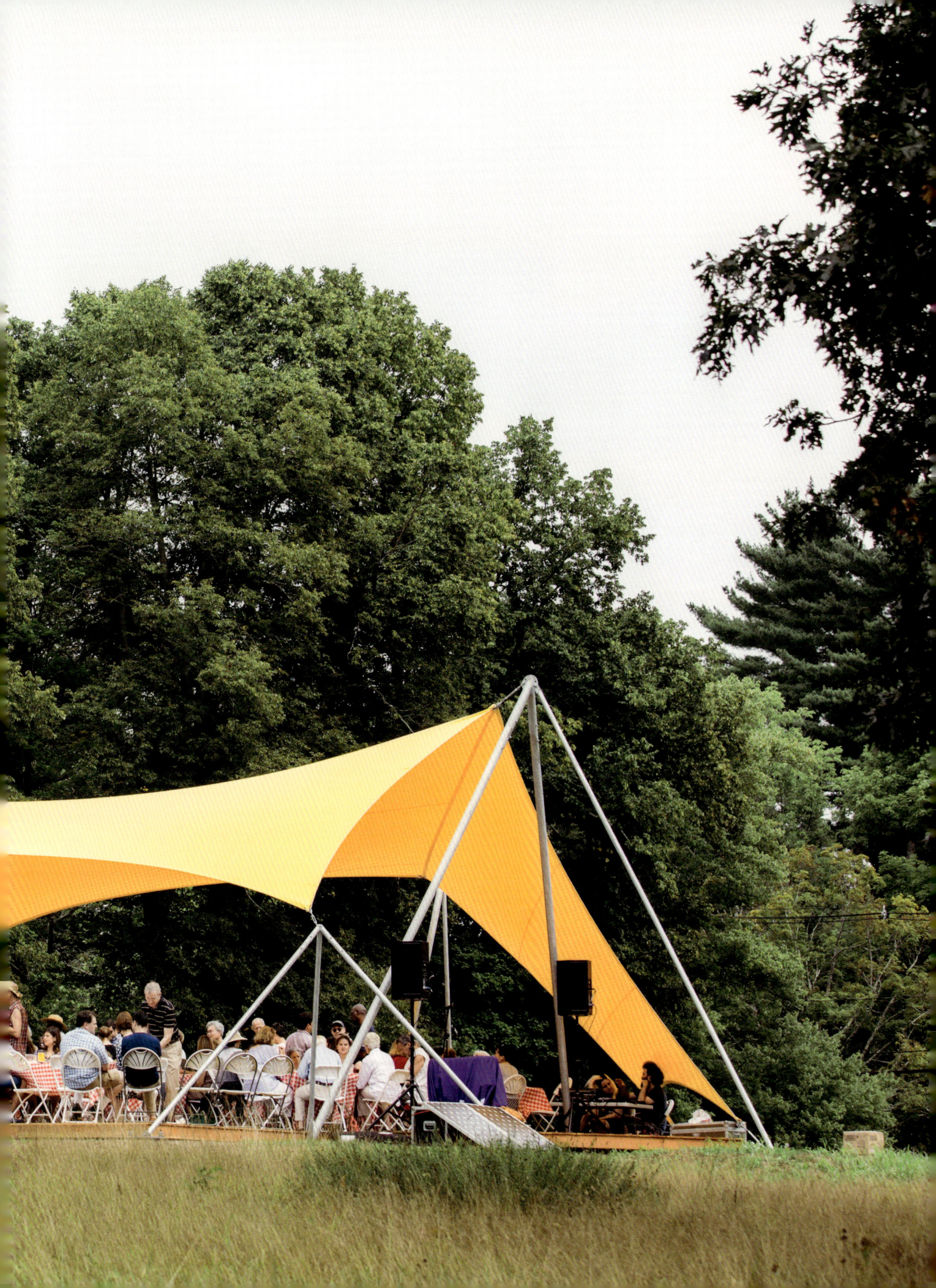

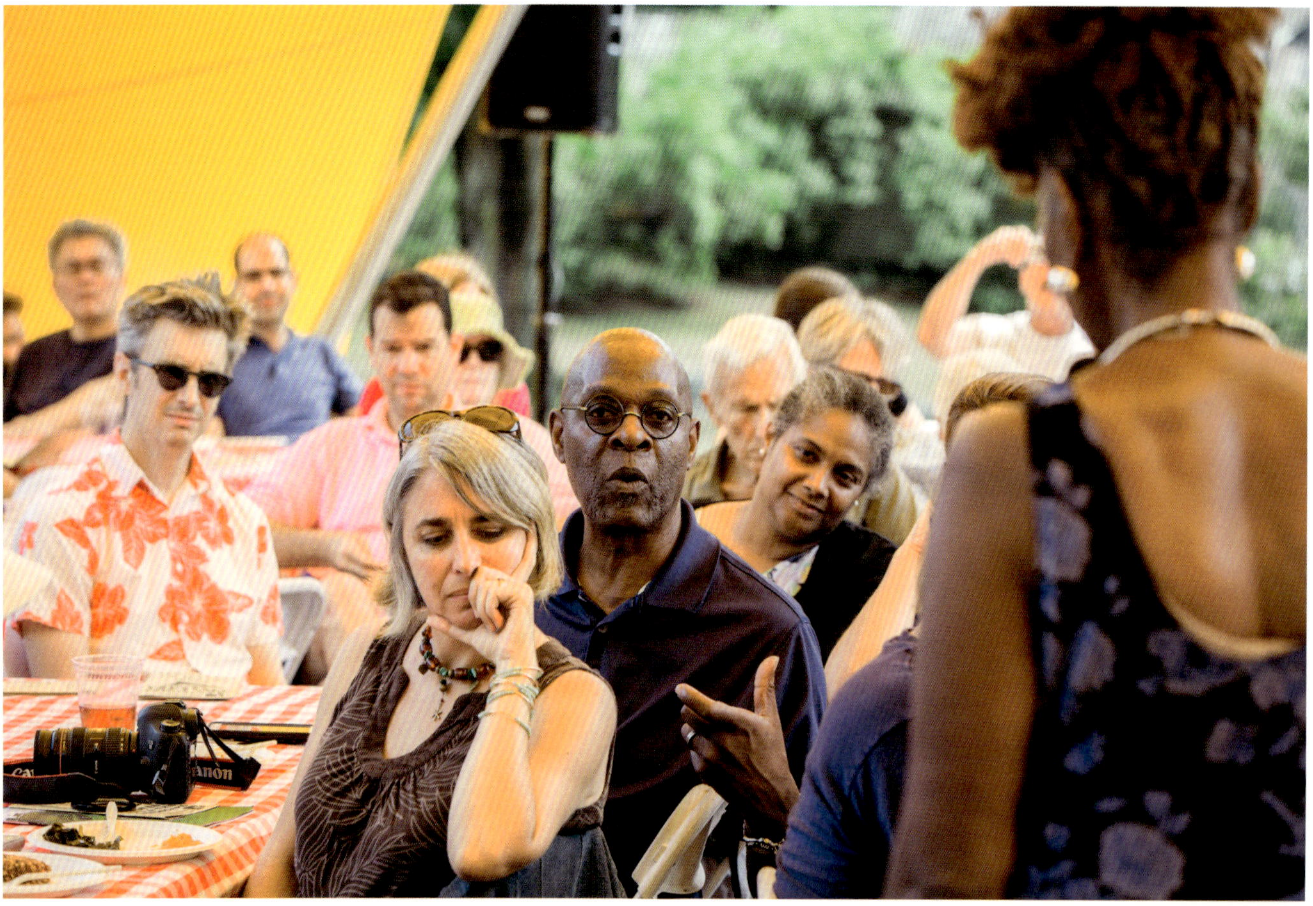

Lyceum I: Fulani Haynes speaking in forefront, facing away from the camera.

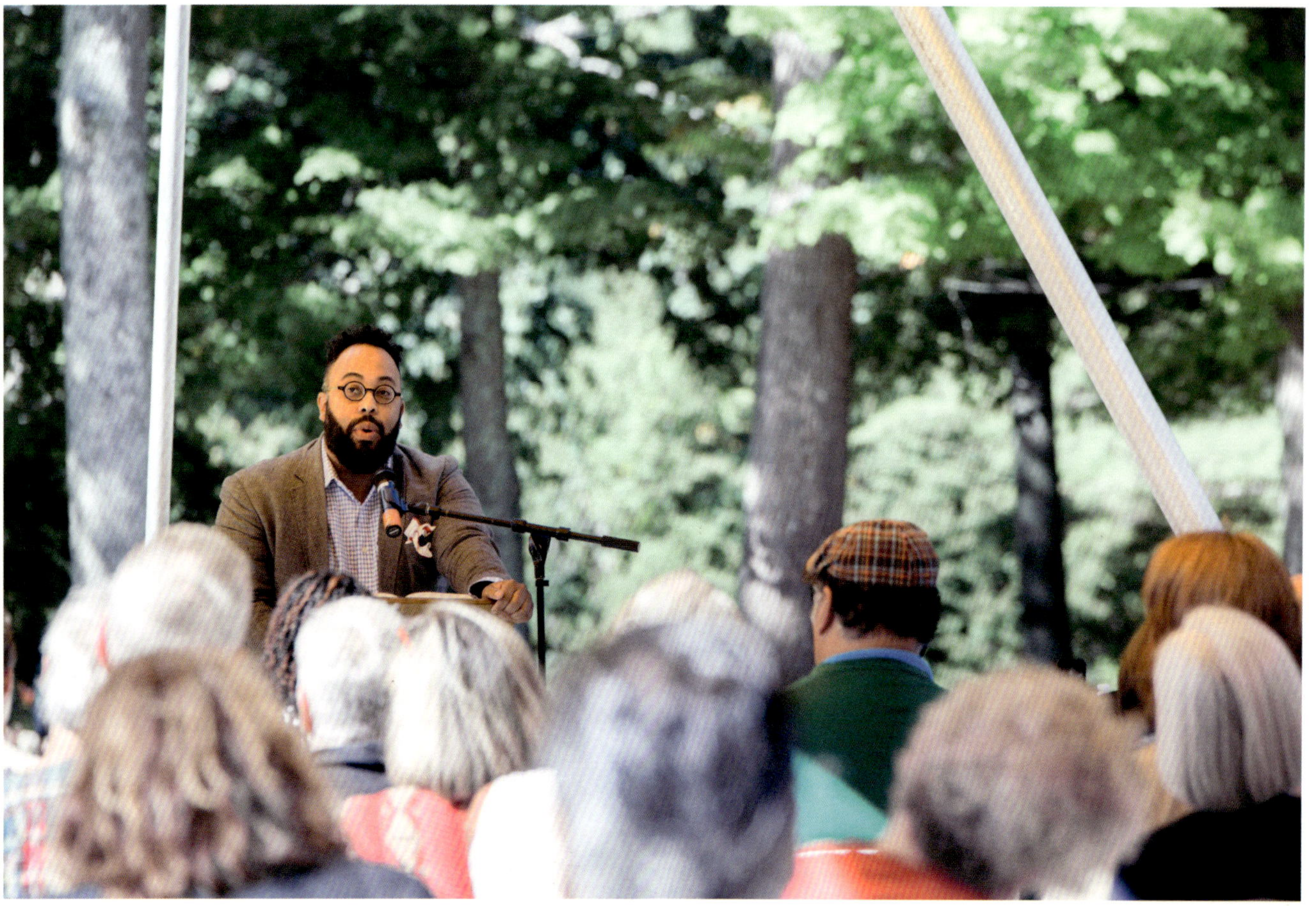

Lyceum II: Kevin Young on stage.

Sam Durant

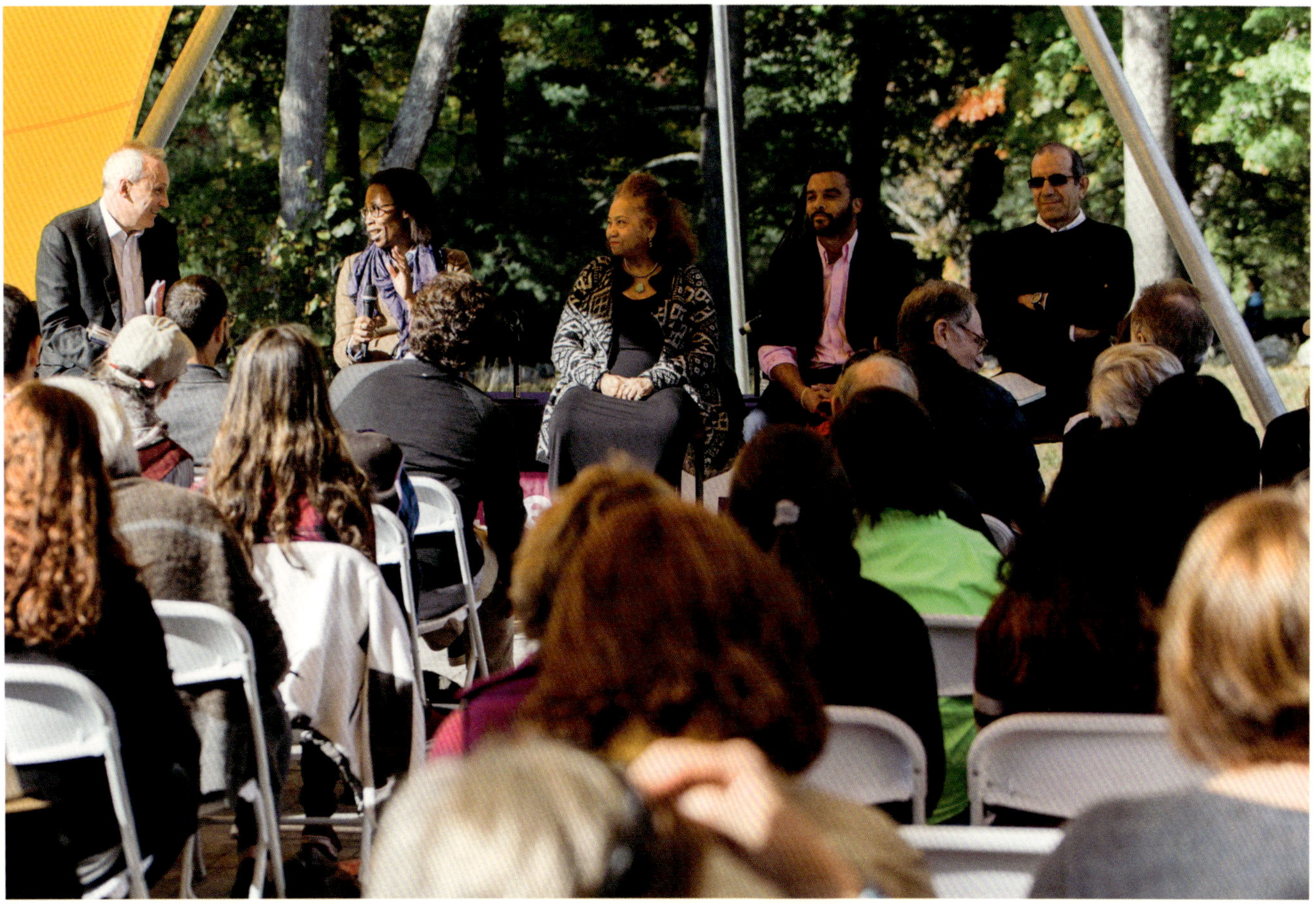

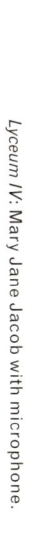

Lyceum III: On stage from left: Tim Phillips, Penny Outlaw, Barbara Lewis, Adam Foss, and Gilead Sher.

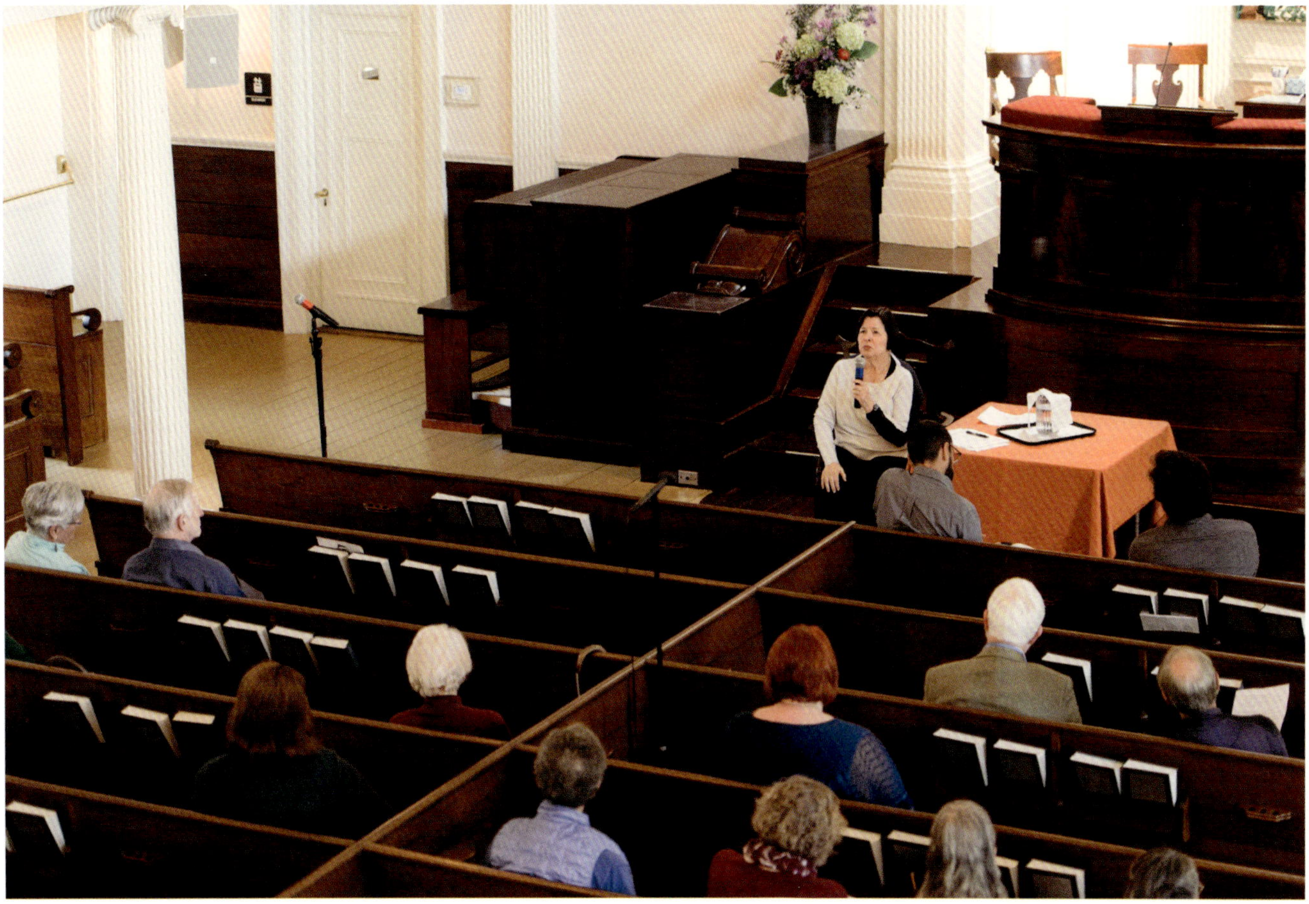

Lyceum IV: Mary Jane Jacob with microphone.

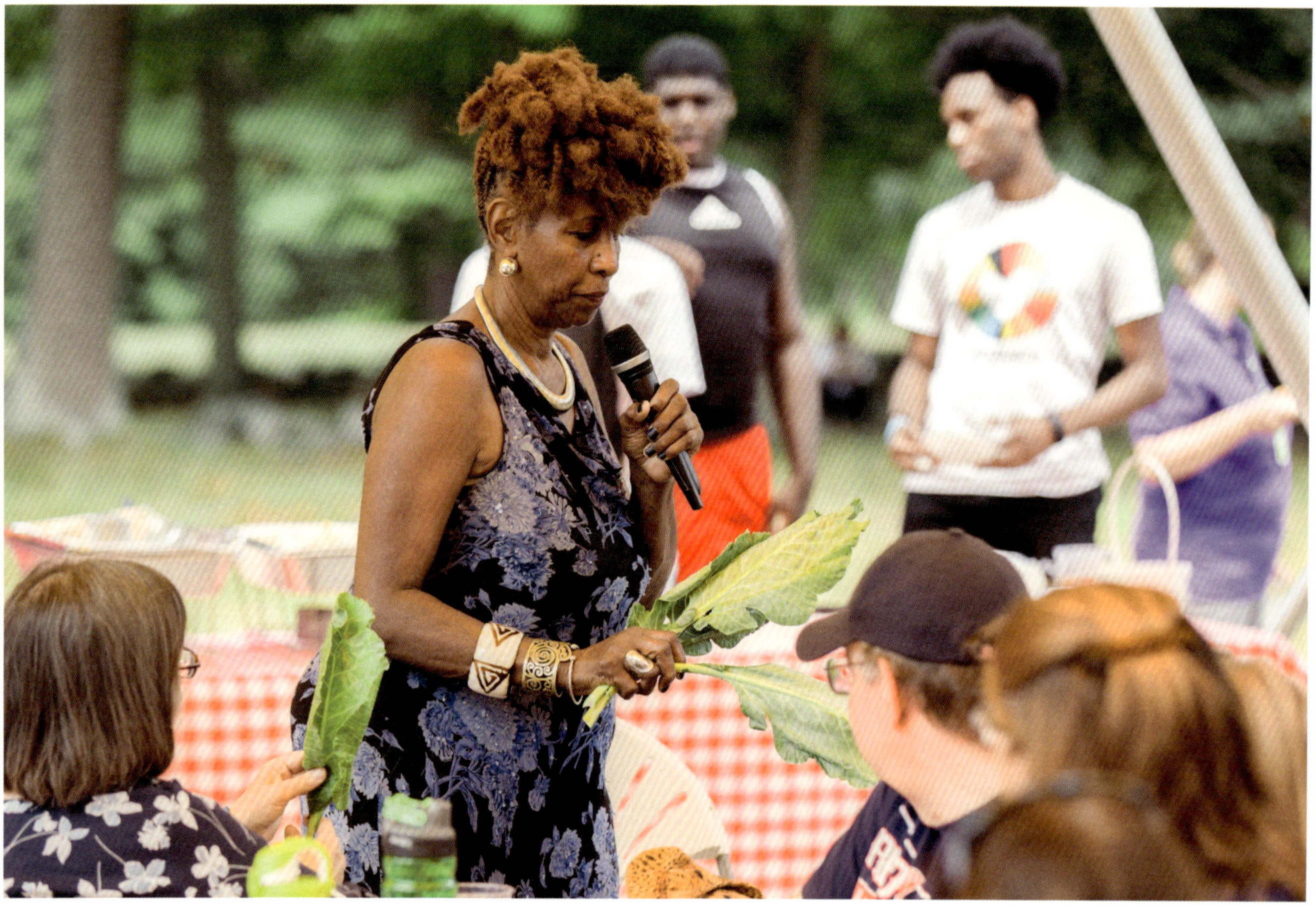

Lyceum I: Fulani Haynes speaking.

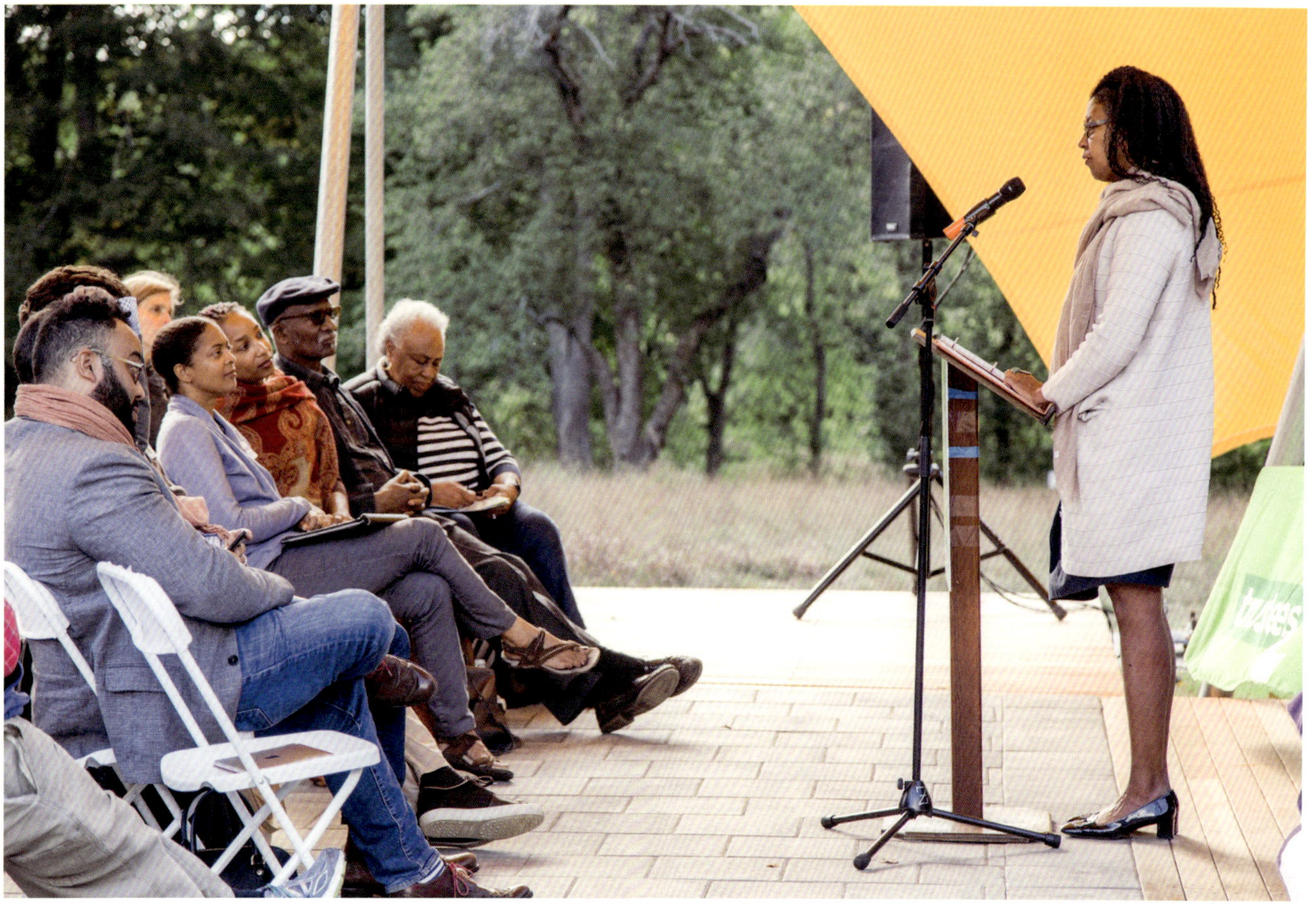

Lyceum II: Robin Coste Lewis at podium.

Sam Durant

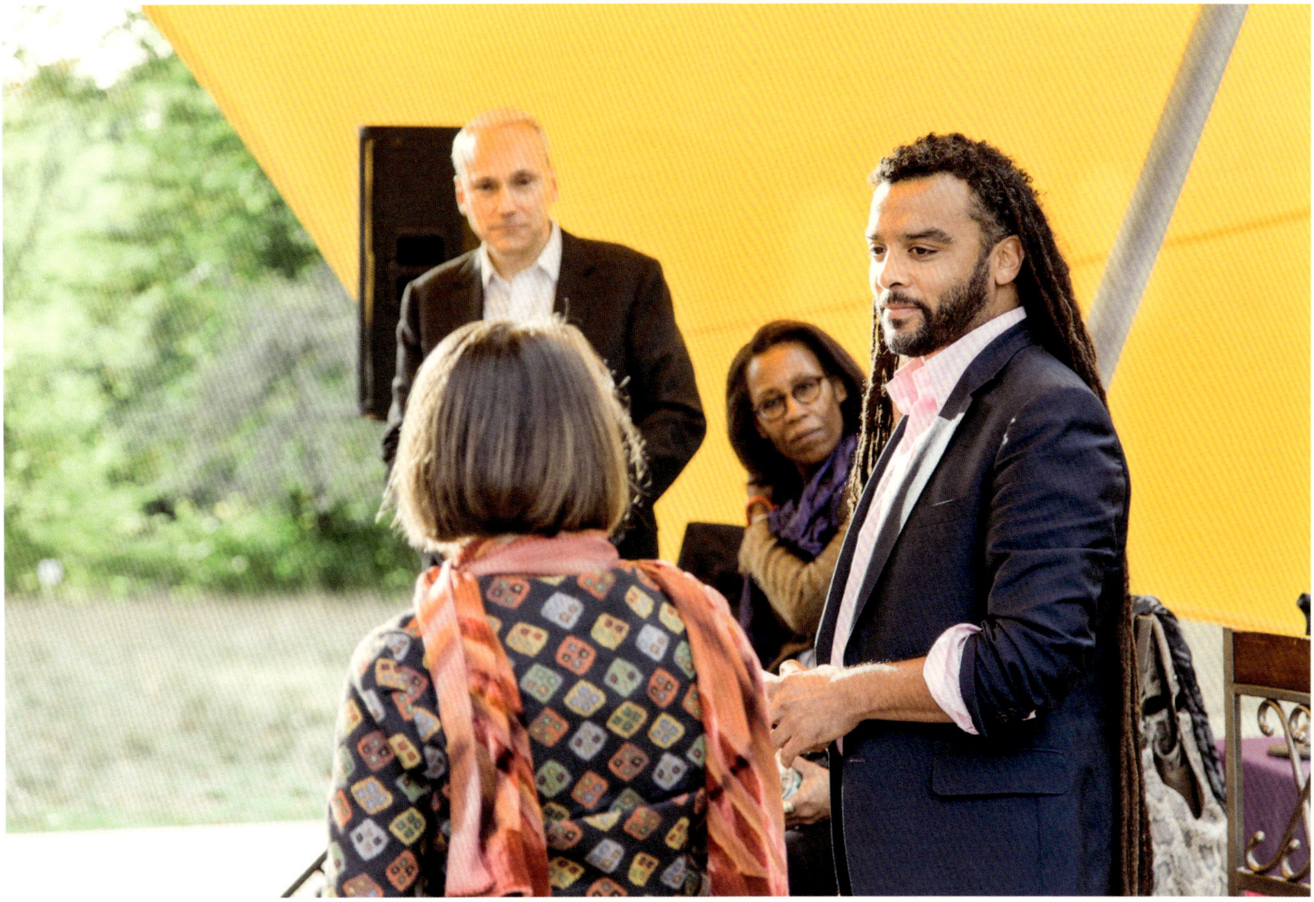

Lyceum III: Tim Phillips, Penny Outlaw, and Adam Foss facing a member of the audience.

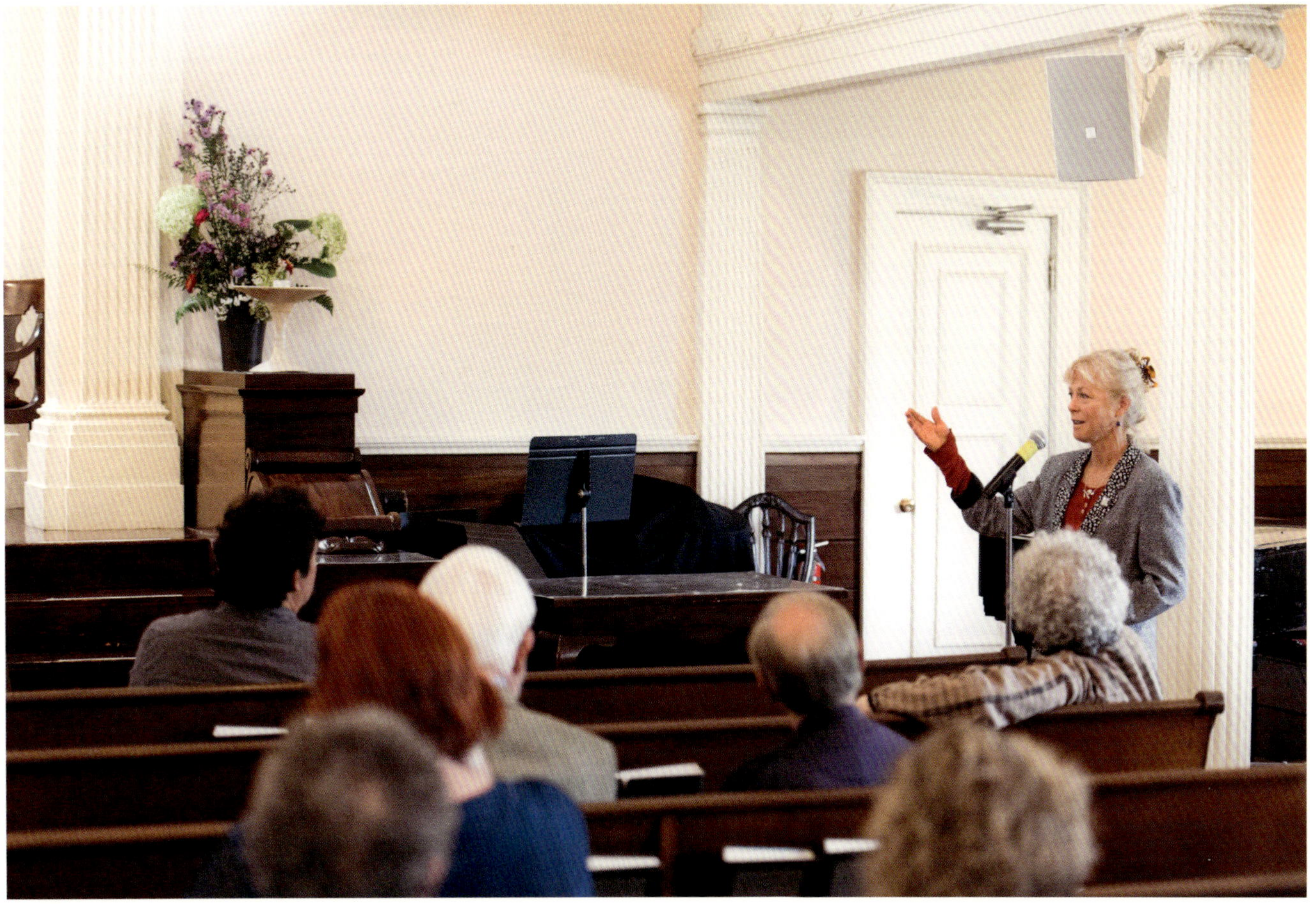

27

Lyceum IV: Audience member speaking at the *New England Town Hall Meeting.*

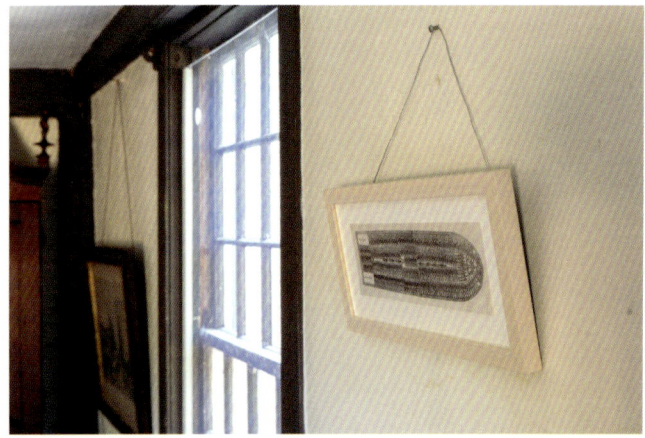

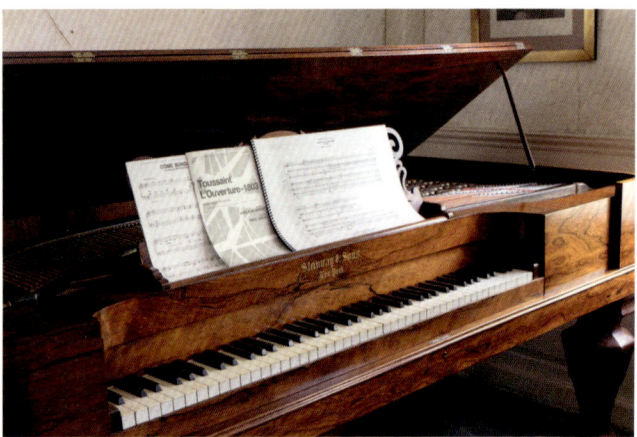

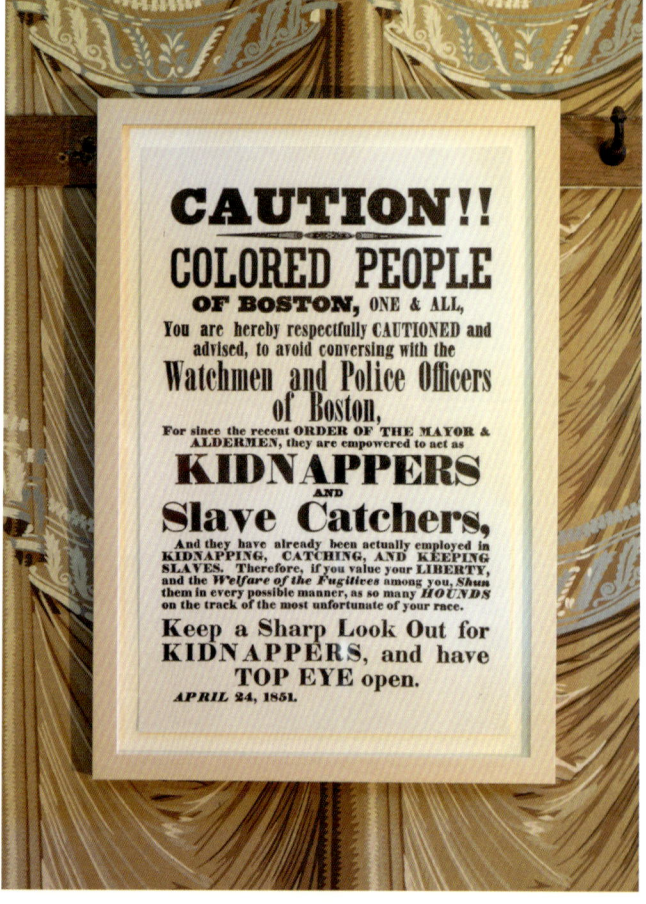

28

From top left

1 Downstairs parlor: Reprinted diagram of human cargo on the British slave ship Brookes.

2 Downstairs music room: Scores from notable African American composers on Sophia Ripley's piano, including *Come Sunday* by Duke Ellington, *Toussaint L'Ouverture, 1803* by Hale Smith and *Dialectics for Two Grand Pianos* by Donal Fox.

3 Front entry hall: Reprint of 1851 Broadside warning Boston's African American community against kidnappers, bounty hunters, and police after the passage of the Fugitive Slave Act.

4 Upstairs hall: Interpretation of a billy club used by African American self-defense groups in the wake of the Fugitive Slave Act. The groups followed strict rules forbidding the use of lethal weapons while battling heavily armed bounty hunters, militias, and police in defending and freeing African men and women escaping bondage.

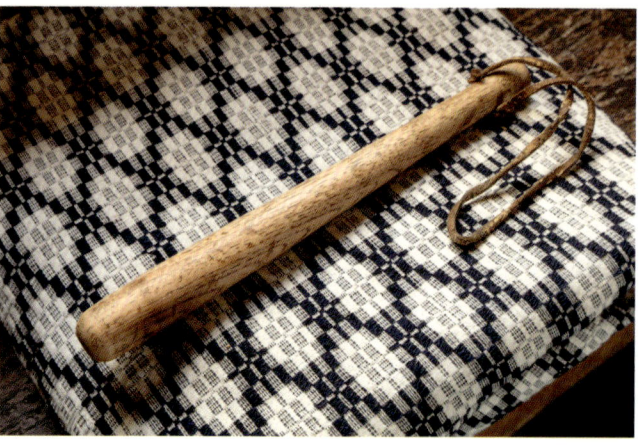

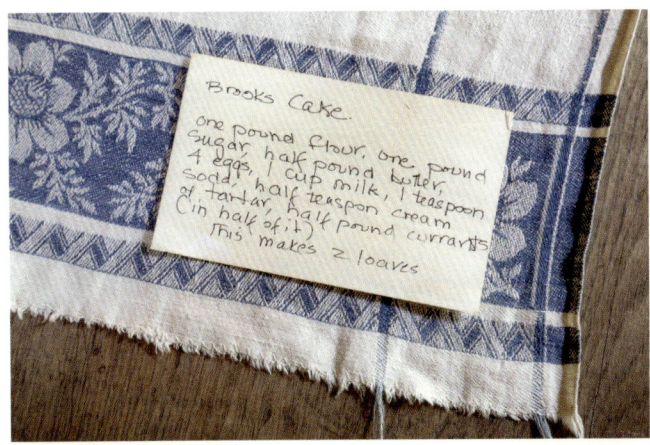

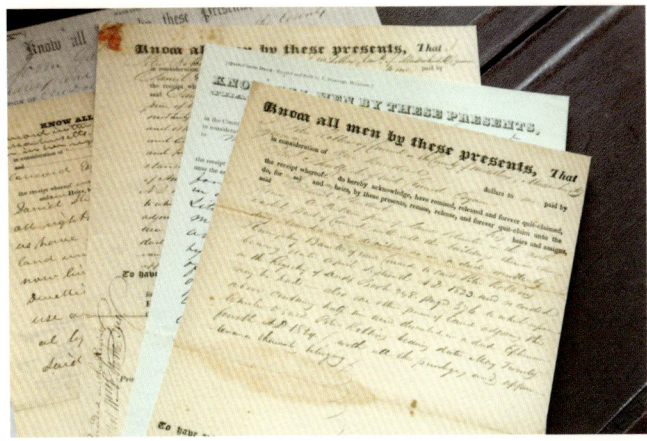

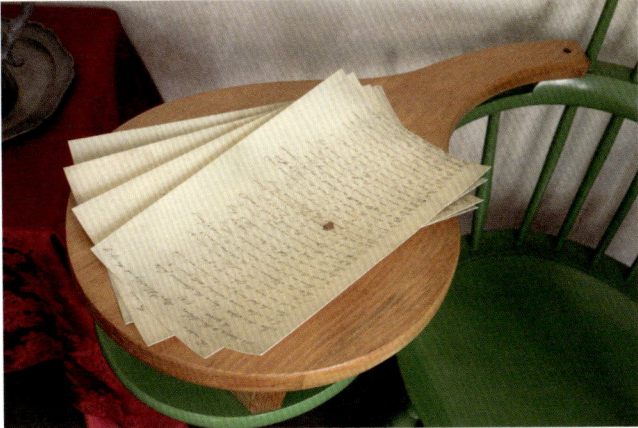

From top left

5 Kitchen: Interpretation of "Brooks Cake" recipe card. The cakes were sold to raise money for the abolitionist movement.

6 Dining room: Reprints of property deeds held by free African men and women in post-revolutionary Concord.

7 Upstairs writing room: Reproduction of Phillis Wheatley poem on the desk of Ralph Waldo Emerson.

8 Side entrance hall: Interpretation of Jack Garrison's walking stick.

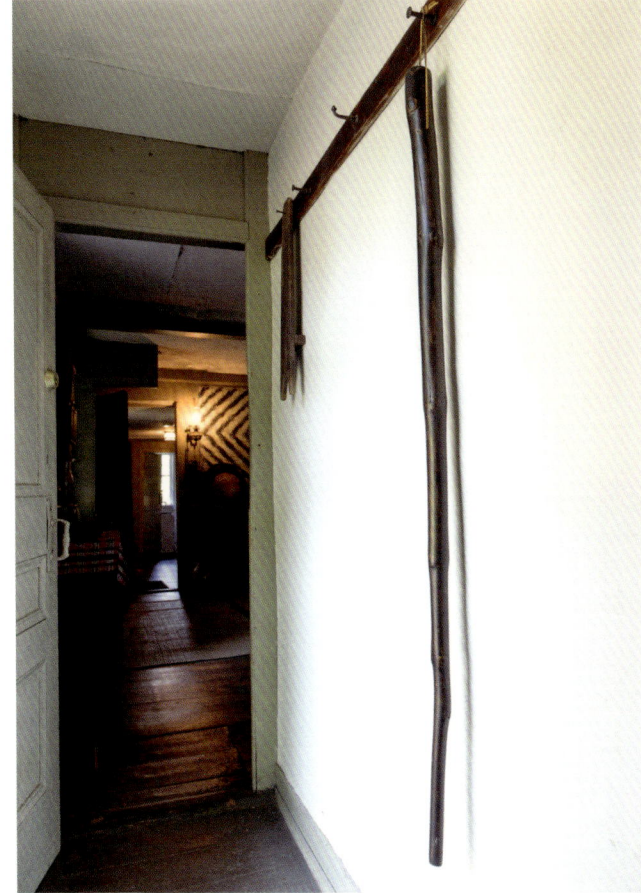

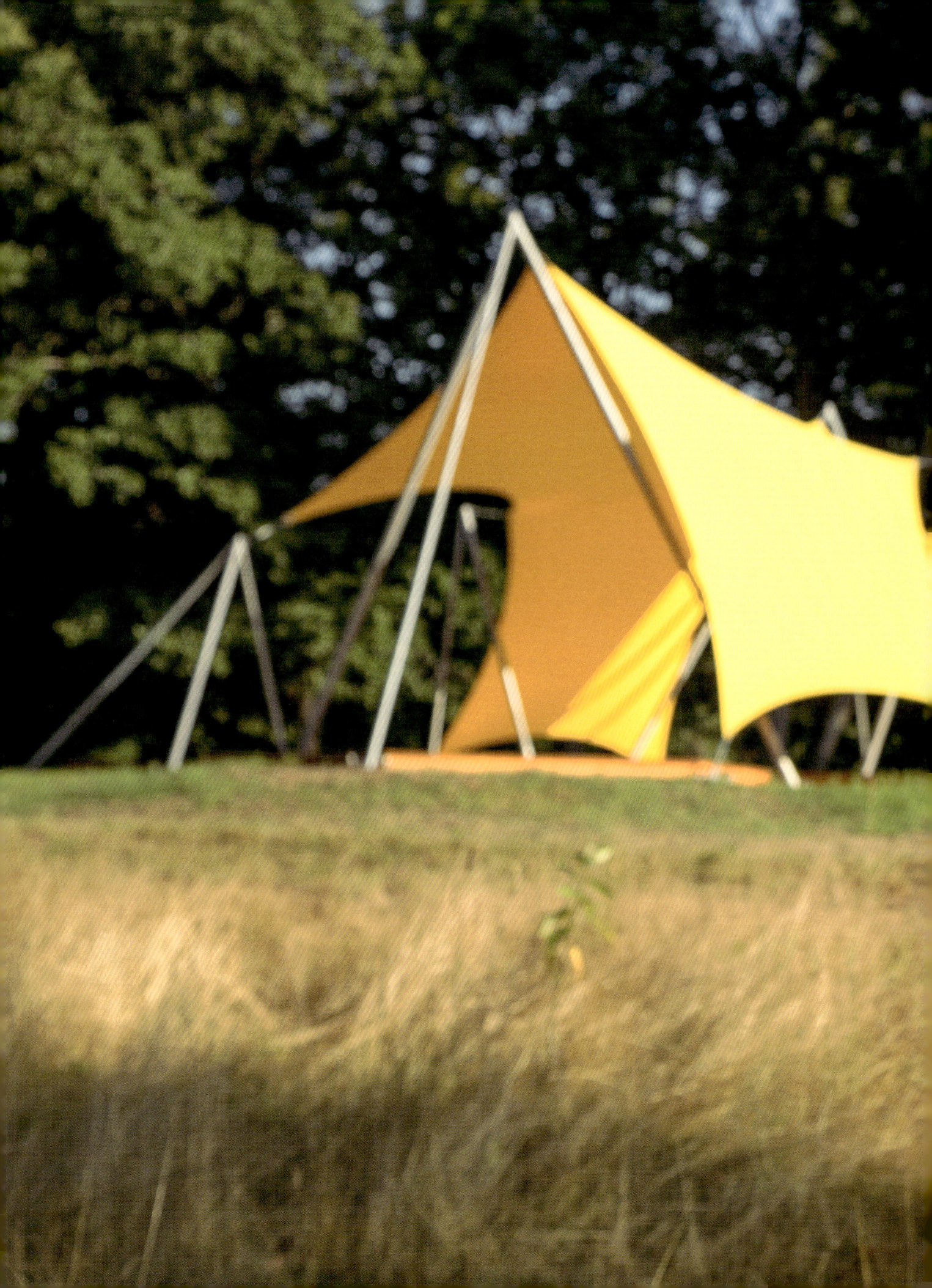

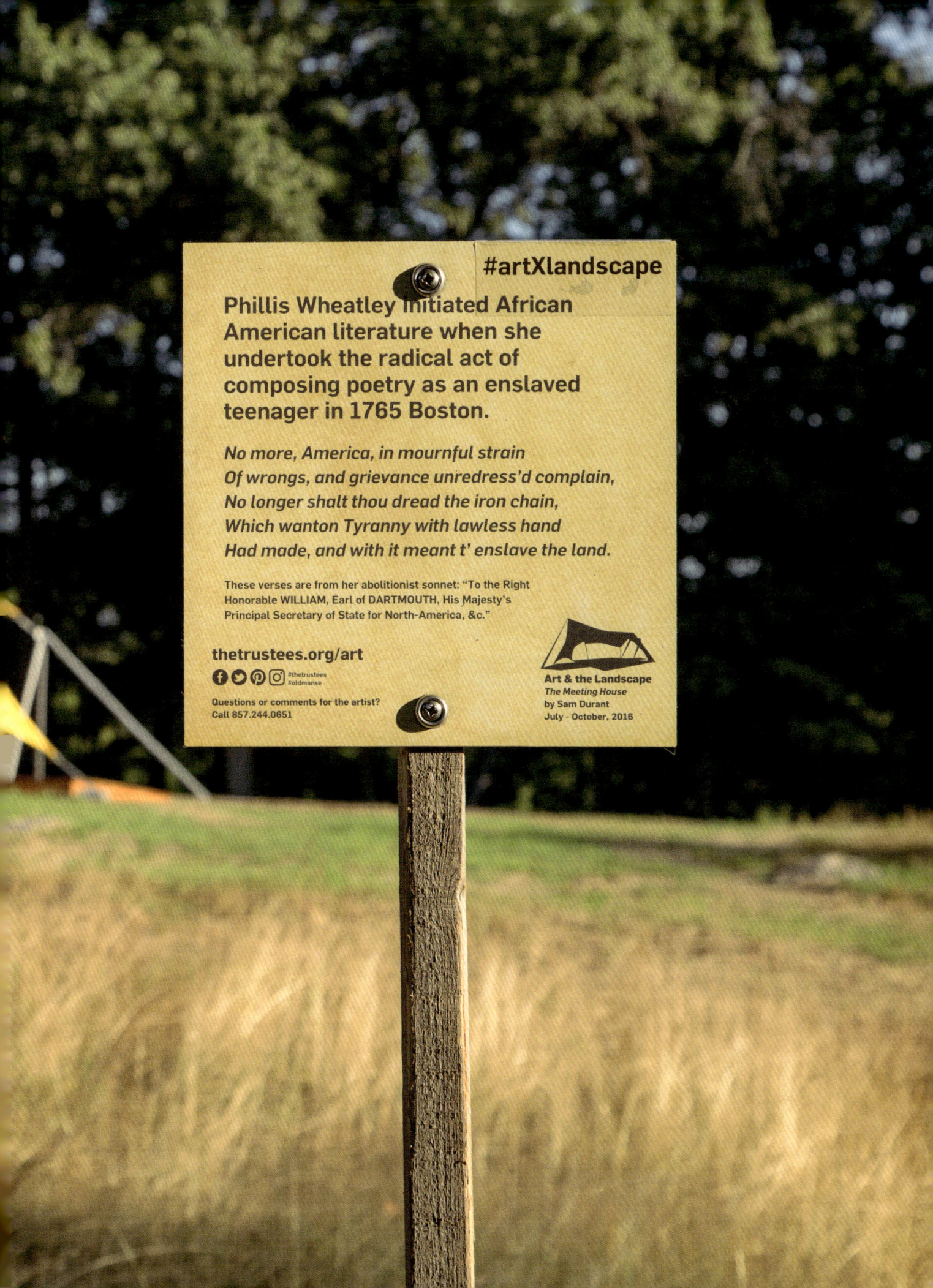

#artXlandscape

Phillis Wheatley initiated African American literature when she undertook the radical act of composing poetry as an enslaved teenager in 1765 Boston.

No more, America, in mournful strain
Of wrongs, and grievance unredress'd complain,
No longer shalt thou dread the iron chain,
Which wanton Tyranny with lawless hand
Had made, and with it meant t' enslave the land.

These verses are from her abolitionist sonnet: "To the Right Honorable WILLIAM, Earl of DARTMOUTH, His Majesty's Principal Secretary of State for North-America, &c."

thetrustees.org/art

#thetrustees
#oldmanse

Questions or comments for the artist?
Call 857.244.0651

Art & the Landscape
The Meeting House
by Sam Durant
July - October, 2016

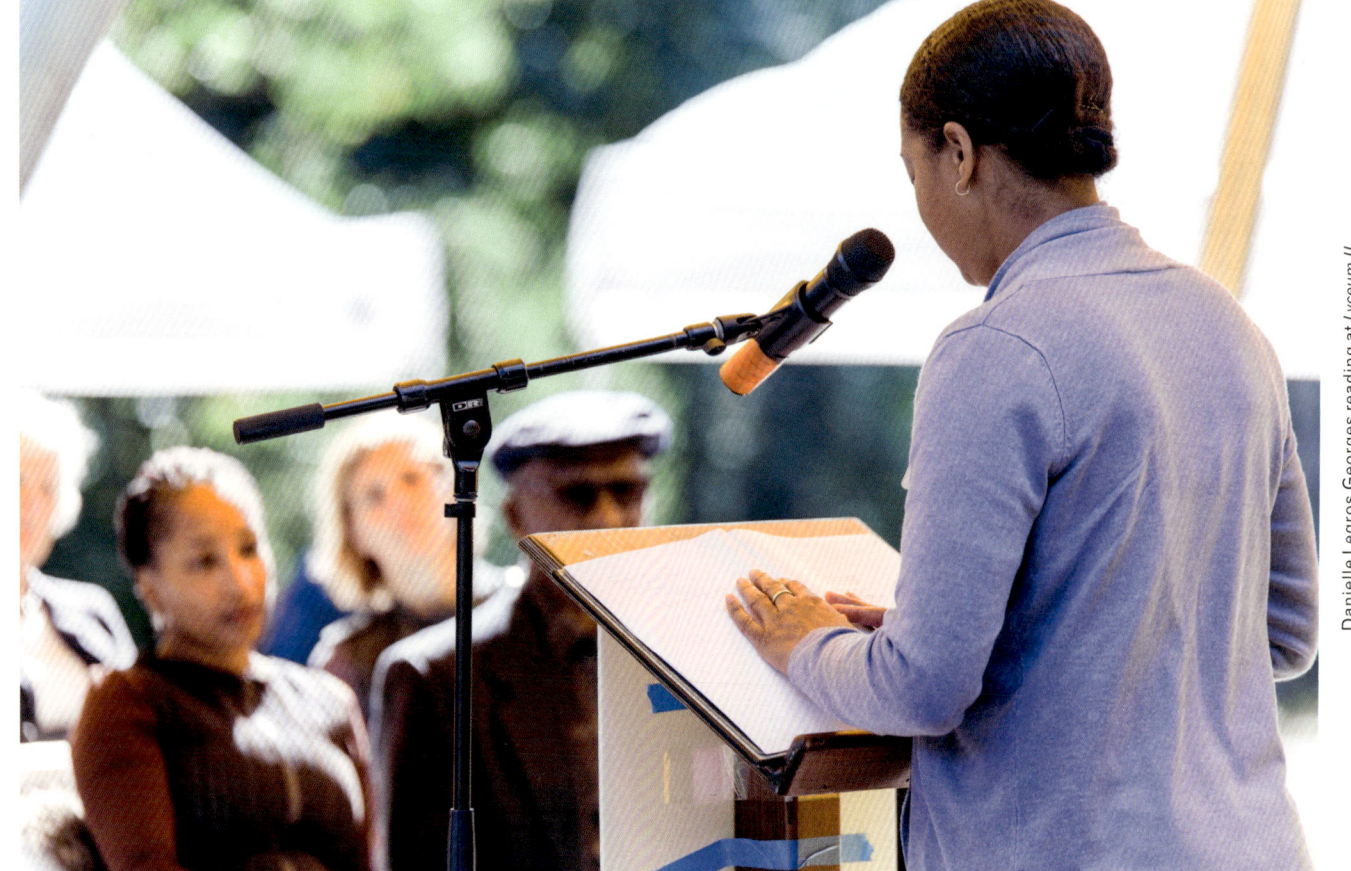

Danielle Legros Georges reading at *Lyceum II*.

Sam Durant

Poetry at The Meeting House

The Old Manse, Concord, Massachusetts
September 24, 2016

Tisa Bryant

Tisa Bryant

After Images

Four ekphrastic* prose poems for *The Meeting House*
installation at The Old Manse by Sam Durant.

*******Ekphrasis** or ecphrasis (adjectival form, ekphrastic), is a graphic, often dramatic, verbal description of a visual work of art, either real or imagined, produced as a rhetorical exercise, understood to stand alone as a work of art in its own right. The term is derived from Plato's dialogues in the *Republic*. The four prose poems presented here are based on the author's photographs and memories of visiting *The Meeting House*, The Old Manse, The Robbins House, and environs, save in one case, "To Remain," in which the author superimposes images from *Auto da Fé*, John Akomfrah's filmic history of forced migrations, onto snapshots of the landscape of the historic home.

Dazzle Camouflage
After the kitchen wallpaper at The Old Manse

We saw some men and women, who had long ago come out, going in *once more through the free and hospitable portals of the Lyceum.*
The way graphically directed in charcoal chevrons artfully smudged along the kitchen walls. What would be inserted has fallen over. A procession of carats on end. The wayside pointed. To the heavy white wood plank door fixed shut. Less than, less than, the sign small and growing larger. Pointing to the window ablaze with early autumn light, facing the fields, the wood beyond. In the center of the room, the table eternally set, bowl, wood plate, white cloth printed with blue flowers, hearth decorative but cold, copper bedwarmer on the andiron. From here, Rev. Emerson witnessed the battle on the Old North Bridge. Sound shocked into silence, the elision heard round these parts. *What should concern Massachusetts is not the Nebraska Bill, nor the Fugitive Slave Bill but her own slaveholding and servility.* This wallpaper, a cocked black ell on white, could simply be love. That "like one of the family" kind of love that follows the condition of the mother. From here, we cannot see the graves of those who labored the land in bondage. Imagine the flag, the bronze marker, obelisk forever piercing up. Take the knee there. The marks adorning the walls do not insert the names of enslaved people who could be seen from the kitchen holding a plow or a bridle, or sketches of their faces rendered in graphite on the attic walls. Neither scar nor stare is marked here. Imagine their eyes and wear them. See, the sign, less than, greater than, is neither fact nor artifact of the sentience of this room or that of the people whom it held, not the material order of memory or muscle, but simply an unfortunate image seized upon, forced into service, uncanny. Like the zebra, each of whose markings are of singular design that when herded form a cosmology, making it difficult for a predator to discern how many of them are there. Dazzle camouflage. As in the history of forcibly moved bodies, or the psyche of wallpaper. Is it the dark marks that record presence, or the spaces between them that matter to the count.

Tisa Bryant

To Remain
After John Akomfrah's film *Auto da Fé*

Enter the frame with claves, with coconut shells clapped together, a woman's spool-heeled shoe against stone. Ox blood. Stepping the measure. She walks along the perimeter of what's left of a house, arms out at her sides. Foundation breaching soil, a lidless box emptied of treasure. Where there is value there is preservation. Where there is value there is memory. Where there is value there is this visitation. She walks along the perimeter, hands crossed at her sternum, her straw hat pinned to her coiled braids. She walks along the perimeter, clutching her purse at her waist with both hands, the hem of her mauve skirt floating above stone, anemone over reef.

She steps along the retaining wall, hands at her sides, purse at her left knee, walking the plank to an unseen ocean, crossing the threshold of the portal. A migration of invisible force. She is one woman. She is four, and more. They walk singly. They walk simultaneously. Their heels meter the erratic times. They stand in a phalanx of echoes, left hands blades slicing air in synchronic movement: left eye, right elbow, left knee, slicing the air. Left eye, right elbow, left knee. A regiment of spells for the sovereign interior. Through the trees, a house rolls on logs, compact, transformed from residence to relic as it emerges from just beyond a field. Behind it, a procession, silent, sweeping the ground before them at each step. Spirit writing. Semaphore.

The women mark the direction. Eye. Elbow. Knee.

We pan the grounds, whispering Royall, Codman, Robbins, Hutchinson, Garrison.

He stands between river and field, his suit the color of sand, his dark pink tie, the deeply tanned leather of his valise saturating our eyes. He is a conch shell. The sky is the sea. He raises his arms, palms cupped. He crosses his wrists above his head, hands fists. He turns and walks to the boathouse, stands at the launch, his colors in relief against the river still as glass.

We turn to the women in a sweep of flight. Flock. Akimbo. Ascend. Eye, elbow, knee. Some are for greater than, greater than, greater than this.

The Mark of Elision
After Elise Lemire's *Black Walden*

Captain John Codman's slave, Mark, had poisoned him. The judge of Concord could not discern the reason why

Phillis, when asked how long she had served Codman, said he'd purchased her when she was a little girl. She says nothing more about who held her close before this.

In April 1740, William Wilson of Concord sold to Sarah Melvin of Concord a two year-old "negro girl" named Nancy.

In April 1752, farmer Henry Spring of Weston sold to Peter Hubbard of Concord a six-ish year-old boy named Cato.

Judge Russell himself had taken one of his slave women's children to Timothy Wesson, who in turn had given Brister to John Cuming, of Concord.

Such was the season, the spring yields of the region.

Common as rye.

Plentiful as air.

But poison?

Nothing could explain it.

Belinda remembered life on the Rio da Valta, where "mountains covered the spicy forests," and she was snatched from a sacred grove where she and her parents performed their devotions. The intruders wrenched her away. Yet after seventy years enslaved at the Royall estate in Charlestown, MA, Ghana never faded from her mind.

Robin Vassall was born to enslaved people on the Royall estate. He, his mother, and his five siblings were inherited by Penelope Royall when Isaac Royall, her father died. The bonds of one family rent those of another. Penelope Royall married a Jamaican planter living in Cambridge, taking Robin, his mother and siblings with her, but leaving behind, with Isaac Royall Jr., eighteen other people who were his inheritance, including Robin's father. Robin's portal to the Lyceum: arsenic. Spirited from a doctor's cache.

Mark was separated from his wife and children in Boston, at the end of February, before spring could even arrive. He remembered his abduction from his country. He remembered his infant son given away to a family in another county. The wrongs against him, against any of them, evidence of nothing at all. Meeting Robin behind a house, under cover of darkness, Mark obtained a packet of poison to end John Codman's tyranny.

As whole families of enslaved and free Black people in this region died of disease born of malnutrition.

Nothing could explain the slaves' plot to burn an entire city of plantations in Antigua, which the Royall, Vassall and other planter families fled to New England to escape. They ran from it, but were still in it. Were the "it" itself and couldn't see it. What their legacy and all it entailed was dependent upon, was nothing without.

Nothing could explain the desperation of slaves. Family was the domain of ownership, the naming of that ownership the classic mark of educated gentlemen. Phoebe. Venus. Phyllis. Cato. Maro. The classical nature of love and deprivation. Their own—whose?—to mourn and to burn.

Tisa Bryant

The Mirrored Stair
After touring the Robbins/Hutchinson House

They shared the house but were not of the same mind.
One family faced west, you could say the New World. You could say the field. You could
say the hand that teaches. The other family faced east, you could say Timbuktu. You could
say fraught. You could say the eye that directs. Between them, a mirror of stairs, the only
likeness their households shared. And the children. Wait. The children. The West family
believed in the salvation of labor. The East, in liberation by the book. They coexist and
cooperate aware of this Imaginot line dividing their visions of the future. Decades and
decades before Booker T. Washington and W. E. B. Du Bois, this wrassling over the vault
to heaven on earth. On one side, now, exhibits of deeds, actions and decrees about the
Robbins' land, Caesar Robbins' mark, an X, as signature, photographs of fields, the rye
cradle, maps and plots of acreage. On the other side, now, in the place where she was
born and raised, Ellen Garrison's story of education and activism, the texts she studied,
the letters she wrote for support of her schooling of Black children. Unifying the sides, the
mirror flight of stairs, which each night the children climbed, mimicking each other's moves,
one foot up, then the other, the only way to climb, and slept aloft together, sharing the yield
that was themselves in the shadow of their parents' choices. I imagine the closeness of their
heads, the fervor of their whispers, the knowing they shared of marking out one's name, of
harvesting rye, of the saga of their family line, the running and reading that freed them and
kept them still, from pallet to pallet, what they shared at night. I remembered being a child in
Dorchester, near Codman Sq., sprawled out on the floor with my brother and cousins while
my parents, aunt and uncle, played bid whist in the kitchen and argued about bussing. My
parents sent us to schools in Newton through METCO; my aunt and uncle were vehemently
opposed. We children huddled together, eyes following the rise and fall of voices along
the walls, whispering of karate lessons and dreidels, comic books and standing alone at
the bus stop in the mornings, winter dark. "We should go to our own schools in our own
neighborhoods." "We deserve the best education, wherever it is." To stay Black, to *be* Black.
Clubs were trump, not spades, not hearts. They partnered in opposition to where the future
lay waiting in the gulf between then, now and forever. In the cleaving of class, race, where
we put our bodies, where we used our minds. "Help me out, partner." "This is all I can do
right now." "Stop talking the board." Our parents got tight and the game got heated. We
listened, wide-eyed to the grunt and hiss of it as the smoke rose above the bloom of their
hair, as the Cutty Sark crackled with ice, as they leaned forward, hungry, in turn, and cut
each other's books.

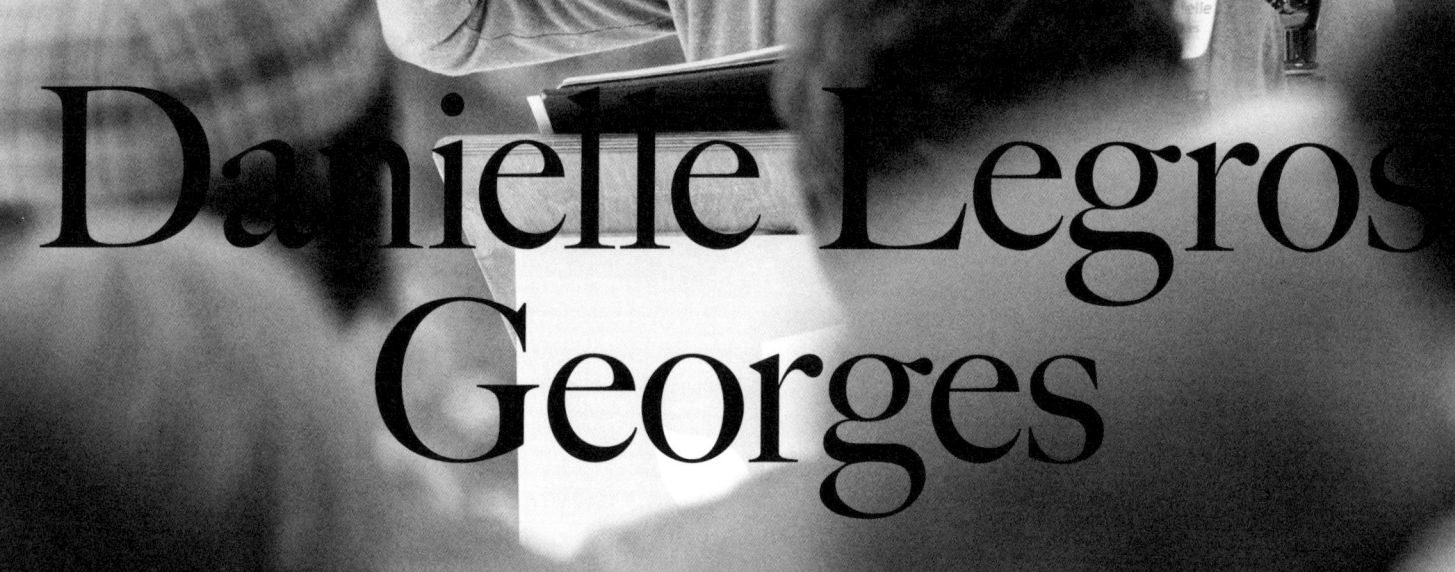

Danielle Legros Georges

Danielle Legros Georges

Acts of Resistance to New England Slavery by Africans Themselves in New England

Self-emancipation by
Walking into the blackest night
Becoming the river
Running into the text

Acquiring a fine English as a Second Language
As a third, a fourth, a fifth

Filing for one's freedom in the courts of Massachusetts
In the courts of New Hampshire
In the courts of Rhode Island
In the court of one's mind
In the court of one's body
Through the course of one's body
Through the course of one body
And the newness of the day

Feigning fullness
With child
Loving one's child
Killing one's child with the red hand of Salvation
Killing one's owner

Working slowly
Spreading rumors
Breaking tools

Dancing how you know
Orishas on the shoulders

Marrying

Disappearing into another self
Disappearing into another race
Witnessing   Never saying
Tarrying and Suicide
Spying   Telling the Truth
Sowing it

Reading
Writing

Declaring *Dignity* and *Beauty*

And *Sordid Avarice*

    Uttering: *Our wretchedness in consequence of slavery*
                Our wretchedness in consequence of ignorance
                Our wretchedness in consequence of the preacher of the religion of jesus christ
                Our wretchedness in consequence of the colonizing scheme

Setting fire to the house

Walking a ruin of cinders

                                    Testifying

Buying oneself
Owning property   Living
Buying kin
Living

                                    Living

42

Note: Poem contains words (italicized) from and titles of the four articles of *David Walker's Appeal to the Coloured Citizens of the World* (1829).

Oral Exam

Phillis Wheatley before her examiners
coaxes the myths from their day-beds.
Retrieves the crescent moon, places

it in the palms of their hands. Draws
the stars she beheld on the deck
of the ship Phillis as she left

its depths. Seized as Persephone
from the earth. *Which is the dark?*
And *What the light? Where the land*

devoted to the God of day may be
the questions to determine this girl
is not a talking dog, a fanciful parrot

from whom divine sound spills
like a glowing ember. *Which gods*
act as gods, and which as mere

mortals? What query hangs like ice
in air to be dissolved in her gaze?
Now she binds Reason and Doubt.

Transects the great chain of being.
The very stake of this. Awake
in the flare of an amassed awareness.

In the systems of revolving worlds.

I am thinking at once *orisha,*
as many as one can dream of
plus always one more.

I am thinking the flight home.
The angel Jibreel's six hundred
wings.

The Senegambian stars.

A mother's libation to the rising sun
as an exuberant fragment of memory.

Of 7 as the number of original years
before the looping and infinite 8.

The 8 that returns us to the room.
To the 18 noteworthy men in question.

And Phillis before them
moving heaven and earth.

44

Note: The phrase *devoted to the God of day* is drawn from Phillis Wheatley's "Reply to the Answer in our last by the Gentleman in the Navy" (*Royal American Magazine*, 1775) and *the systems of revolving worlds* from her poem "To the University of Cambridge, in New England" (*Poems on Various Subjects, Religious and Moral*, 1773).

Poem as Bill of Sale and Site of Stifled Rage and Sorrow

Bill of Sale for Enslaved 2-year-old Girl Violet
(name crossed out and changed to Nancy)

Know all men by these presents that I, William Wilson of Concord in the County of Midd.^{x} of New England Gen.^{t}–for the sum of Thirty Pounds to me secured and payed by Sarah Melvin of Said Concord, Widow. Do hereby fully and absolutely Sell, Grant, Convey, and Passover to said Sarah Melvin, her heirs and assigns for ever a certain Negro girl being a slave about two-years of age called ~~Violet~~ Nancy to be to her, her heirs and Assigns, for her and their use and Service, During the said Negro girl's natural life. Hereby for myself, heirs, Execut.^{rs} and Admin.^{rs} Warranting her said Negro girl to her Said Sarah Melvin, her heirs and Assigns from the legal claims or Demands of any person.

Witness my hand and seal April 22 A.D.1740
Witnesses—
Thomas Jones   William Wilson
Thomas Miles

~~Bill of Sale for Enslaved 2-year-old Girl~~ Baby Violet
(name sustained and repeating many times)

VioletVioletVioletVioletVioletVioletVioletVioletVioletVioletVioletVioletVioletVioletVi
oletVioletVioletVioletVioletVioletVioletVioletVioletVioletVioletVioletVioletVioletViole
tVioletVioletVioletVioletVioletVioletVioletVioletVioletVioletVioletVioletVioletVioletVi
oletVioletVioletVioletVioletVioletVioletVioletVioletVioletVioletVioletVioletVioletViole
tVioletVioletVioletVioletVioletVioletVioletVioletVioletVioletVioletVioletVioletVioletVi
oletVioletVioletVioletVioletVioletVioletVioletVioletVioletVioletVioletVioletVioletViole
tVioletVioletVioletVioletVioletVioletVioletVioletVioletVioletVioletVioletVioletVioletVi
oletVioletVioletVioletVioletVioletVioletVioletVioletVioletVioletVioletVioletVioletVi.

Witness my hand and seal the day she is born
Witnesses—
Mother   Midwife who brings this child into the world

Note: First half of poem consists of "Bill of sale, William Wilson to Sarah Melvin (both of Concord), 1740 Apr. 22," for "a certain Negro girl being a slave about two years of age called Nancy" [the name originally written as "Violet," then crossed through and "Nancy" written above the line], forming part of the collection Bills of Sale for Slaves, by or to Concord, Mass., Residents, 1740–1755 (Vault A50, Unit 1), William Munroe Special Collections, Concord Free Public Library, Concord, Mass.; quoted by permission of the Concord Free Public Library.

Walden Woods

Turn and you will see Brister Freeman
self-styled *man of color* in a field he owns
as he plants the seeds of apple trees that bear

fruit, wild and tart. His wife Fenda nearby
suggests with her name a cleaving, a cracking
open, but repairs the world with the telling

of fantastical fortunes. Thoreau tells us she is
fat and *blacker than any of the children of night,*
that *such a dusky orb as never rose on Concord*

before or since. He is divining, clearly, slipping
backward through time to bring us an image
of those who have lived as he will live:

Bound by the law and beyond bondage.
Facing the woods' twin torments—persistence
and sense, the gods of modest circumstances.

Defiant. Original.

Later and returned to civilized life, Thoreau
will write *some have asked what I got to eat*
in the woods; *if I did not feel lonesome;*

if I was not afraid.

Let's return now to the woods, its small cluster
of outcasts, to the field. See Brister Freeman
self-freed by a war that has fashioned a country.

See him move to slave now in a slaughterhouse,
its meat packed and shipped to the West Indies.
Now in a matrix that will harbor the mills

of a million pounds of cotton fed them
by the far-off plantations of the new nation's
South. In the massive circle of profit and appetite

Danielle Legros Georges

lashing Concord to the ports of the Caribbean,
Concord to the West African coast seething
with barracoons, pens that unmake men,

that strip the names of women from their lips.
See Brister Freeman make up his mind and say:
Land. Land as the greatest god. As the freer of us.
Land at all costs.

Note: Poem is inspired by sections of Elise Lemire's book *Black Walden* (2009).

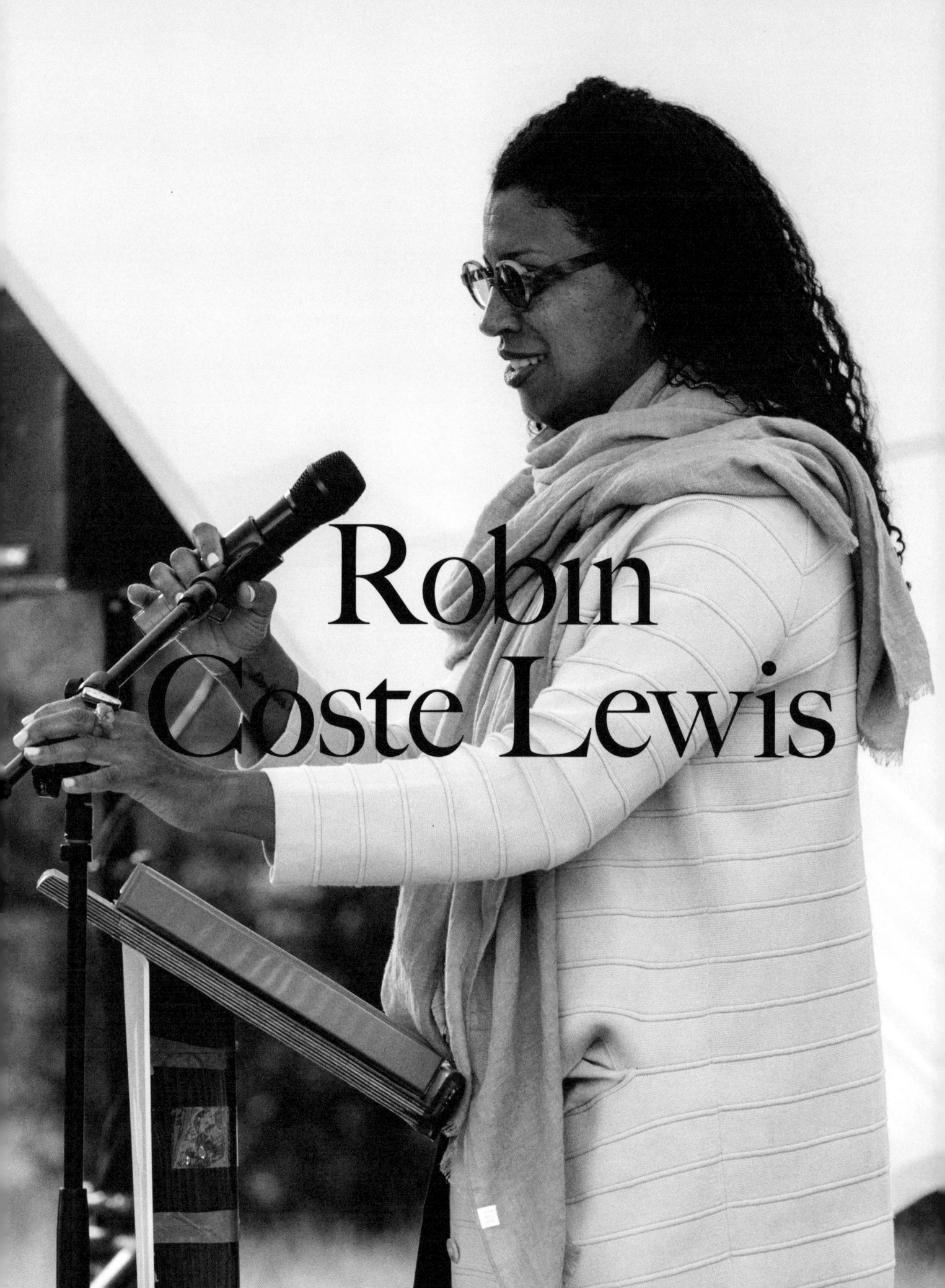

Robin
Coste Lewis

Robin Coste Lewis

"Inhabitants and Visitors"

Note: In 1854, Thoreau published his now canonical *Walden: Or, Life in the Woods.* Well-regarded for its exploration of nineteenth-century subsistence living, Thoreau also included a chapter that explored the community of free Blacks living around Walden Pond long before he arrived. He titled this chapter "Former Inhabitants and Winter Visitors." My poem below is an erasure of Thoreau's chapter. Like Walden at the time of Thoreau's experiment, for me this chapter contained a hidden call to the historical rediscovery of African American histories embroidering Concord, and hence, America. Therefore, in order to extend Thoreau's experiment, I removed and rearranged several lines from Thoreau's chapter in order to magnify, lyrically, the free Black community that once lived there.

In honor of the opening of
The National Museum of African American History and Culture

and

Dedicated to Kevin Young,
with profound admiration,
on the occasion of being named Director of
the Schomburg Center for Research in Black Culture

My fireside,
    My darkline,
        My border-dotted
            dwelling.

My own alone,
    My firm open,
        My across the road,
            My gentle permission.

My narrow present
    half-obliterated fringe
        of now—
            golden, luxuriant.

My still-shrill war
    dwelling on parole—
        Inhumane bricks amid
            the oak copse there.

My discolored emphasis—black,
    blacker than any dusky orb,
        before or since
            My orchard of location.

My-thology
    (Prominent. Astounding.)
        My biography
            (robs and murders

the whole history
    enacted here).
        Let Time intervene
            the most distinct and dubious tradition

50 Saluted—
    standing—
        unoccupied
            election.

My labored lethargy, awake,
    My poetry skipping,
        My bells rung in hot haste.
            Engines fire all together. Fresh sparks.

My ever and anon,
    My cooled ardor
        thought concluded.
            Speaking trumpets,

Passage in the preface,
    The soul's only survivor.
        Heir of burning first moments.
            My gaze, my always, remembered absolutely.

Robin Coste Lewis

My mere presence,
        My dark heaven,
                which could never be burned
                        or mounted.

The iron hook
        hangs history
                (Once more
                        on the left).

My earthen descendants,
        My sufferance,
                My vain form.
                        Midsummer Man carrying a load—

My inquired concern,
        A potter's wheel of him,
                Clay and wheel scripture—
                        An art ever-practiced.

Last inhabitants
        of these woods
                before me,
                        Names with coil,

Civil speech carmine,
        curled up by use—
                The last symbol a dim garden over-run
                        with Roman beggar-ticks.

My dent in the earth,
        This site
                These dwellings:
                        buried cellar stones—

and strawberries,
        thimble-berries,
                hazel-bush,
                        chimney nook,

Sweet-scented black waves
  where the door was sometimes
    the well
      Visible.

Fate, free-will, fore-
  knowledge absolute. Form
    and dialect
      edifying as philosophy.

My vivacious
  lilac generation,
    the door and lintel and sill
      are unfolding.

Plucked by the traveller,
  tended by children
    in front-yard plots
      now standing.

Lone century
  universally thirsty
    making the wilderness
      blossom like the rose:

Deliver me from a city
  built on the site of a more ancient city
    whose materials are ruins,
      whose gardens cemeteries.

My season
  My wanderer
    My house for a week
      or a fortnight at a time

My great snow of 1717
  My long time buried
    without food
      My hole, which the chimney's breath made in the drift.

My house,
  My meandering dotted line,
    Same number of steps, same length,
      coming and going.

Robin Coste Lewis

My own deep tracks,
　　　Heaven's own blue,
　　　　　My deepest appointment,
　　　　　　　My plainly erect neck.

Feathers, lids, winged brother
　　　of the peninsular relation,
　　　　　My nearer approach.
　　　　　　　Impatient

Delicate twilight,
　　　New perch,
　　　　　Peace smitten on one cheek—
　　　　　　　notwithstanding the odor of morale

(Church or State haul
　　　Load of manure
　　　　　Large fires
　　　　　　　Clear when others failed).

My darkness, my lamp
　　　through the trees, like the nut its kernel.
　　　　　Unsuspected faith,
　　　　　　　God of Defaced and Leaning Monuments.

Enter ye
　　　O World behind us
　　　　　Pledge no institution
　　　　　　　whichever way we turn

Blue-robed roof, Mother of pearl flocks,
　　　form and dissolve the fable, every
　　　　　circular inch. Open its seams.
　　　　　　　Long to be remembered.

Expect the Visitor who never comes.
　　　Say, "Remain at eventide,
　　　　　as long as it takes, long enough
　　　　　　　to milk a whole herd of cows."

"Lay Nigh"
An Erasure of Lucy Terry Prince's *Bars Fight*

Note: Lucy Terry Prince was the first known African American to compose a poem on the North American landmass in the late eighteenth century. She lived in Deerfield. The poem was preserved orally for over a century, when it was eventually published in the mid-nineteenth century.

Lay nigh
The names of whom
I'll not leave
Out

His face
His friends
Life so dear

Hope running
Petticoats on the ground

54

Robin Coste Lewis

"Lucy Terry Prince Prepares for Her Marriage"

from "Mr. and Mrs. Prince:
An African American Courtship
and Marriage in Colonial Deerfield"
by Gretchen Holbrook Gerzina

First a fan
Then some pins
and chocolate

Later: five yards of checkered cloth
Cambric

Later still seven shillings of imported linen
More cambric
ribbons

A double-stranded white necklace
More ribbon

A string of beads
A skein of silk thread

thimble
mug
buttons
five yards of galoon

silver or gold trimming

a sheet of drawing paper

Then, in 1751:

3 sheets of paper

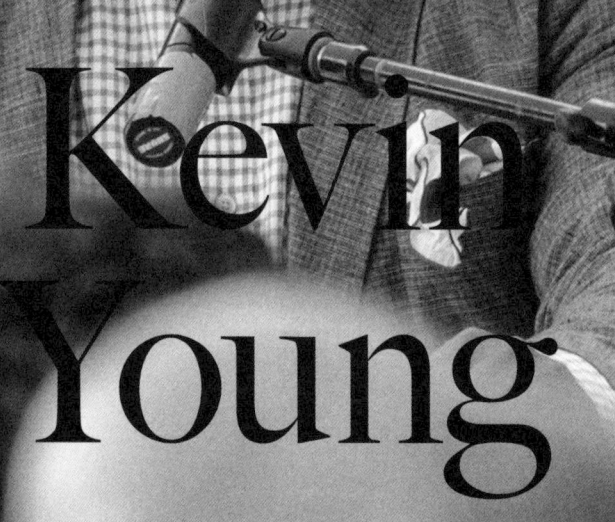

Kevin
Young

A Trinity for Phillis Wheatley

Thou, Phillis, when thou hunger hast,
  Or pantest for thy God;
Jesus Christ is thy relief,
  Thou hast the holy word.

    —Jupiter Hammon

Race in the negro is of appalling importance.

    —Ralph Waldo Emerson
    English Traits

**On the Affray in King-Street,
on the Evening of the 5th of March, 1770**

Why not run? Like young
Crispus Attucks unmoored
from Framingham
to become a dockhand

lugging tea and rum.
Like a mouth his master ran
an ad offering a reward
for his return. Instead,

Attucks, once you're dead,
we will hoist your name
like a flag. The mob
had its orders, attacked,

the king his stones.
The lobster-coats
surely saw you, stevedore,
swaying there—a head taller

than anyone—they'd sparred
with you & others
just days before.
Death no one spares.

I've never heard a black man
loved so, by God—
through the streets
where slaves are sold

your name now rings
out like gold, or coal
whistling in the fire.
One musket ball sped

through your spare rib.
The other through
your true. What all
you left behind:—

58

Kevin Young

this pewter teapot
dry, battered, parched,
without one dark drop.
Adam of us all,

you are buried
on a hill
where the stones
grow slowly small.

An Address to Miss Phillis Wheatley
by Jupiter Hammon

As this Address is wrote in a better Stile
than could be expected from a slave,

some may be ready to doubt of the gen-
uineness of the production. The Author,

as he informs in the title page, is a servant of Mr. Lloyd, and has been remark-

able for his fidelity and abstinence
from those vices, which he warns

his brethren against. The manuscript wrote
in his own hand, is in our possession.

We have made no material alterations
in it, except in the spelling,

which we found needed consid-
erable correction.

    The PRINTERS.
New-York, 20th. Feb. 1787.

60

Kevin Young

A Frieze for Trayvon Martin

Because the night has no
    number, because
the thunder doesn't
    mean rain
Because maybe
    Because we must
say your names
    & the list grows
longer & more
    endless
I am writing this:
    you are no gun
nor holster, no
    finger aimed, thumb
a hammer cocked
    back, all the way—
I refuse
    to bury you, to inter
your name in earth,
    or to burn you back
to bone, to what
    we all know, the soft
song of your skull
    as a child, the place
God or your mother
    or same thing
left untouched
    by hands—
that halo whole
    till they said you weren't—
that Death
    could be your breath—
could be a body
    or less—& you
grew more black
    & blue.
I refuse
    to watch. I refuse.
Not guilty. Not
    guilty. I know you
will stay & rise
    like the sea—

the tide
    all salt & shifting.
Don't ever leave.

Notes

"On the Affray" refers to the Boston Massacre that jumpstarted the American Revolution; its title is taken from the title of Phillis Wheatley's poem about the massacre. The poem first appeared in my *Blue Laws: Selected & Uncollected Poems 1995–2015* as part of "Homage to Phillis Wheatley."

"An Address" takes its title from a tribute poem by African American poet Jupiter Hammon; the poem's body borrows from the introduction to *An Address to the Negroes In the State of New-York,* by Jupiter Hammon, Servant of John Lloyd, jun, Efq; on the Manor of Queen's Village, Long-Ifland, 1787.

"A Frieze for Trayvon Martin" is for him and other contemporary victims of police violence and vigilante justice.

Sam Durant

Build Therefore Your Own World

Blum & Poe, Los Angeles, California
January 7–February 18, 2017

Build Therefore Your Own World

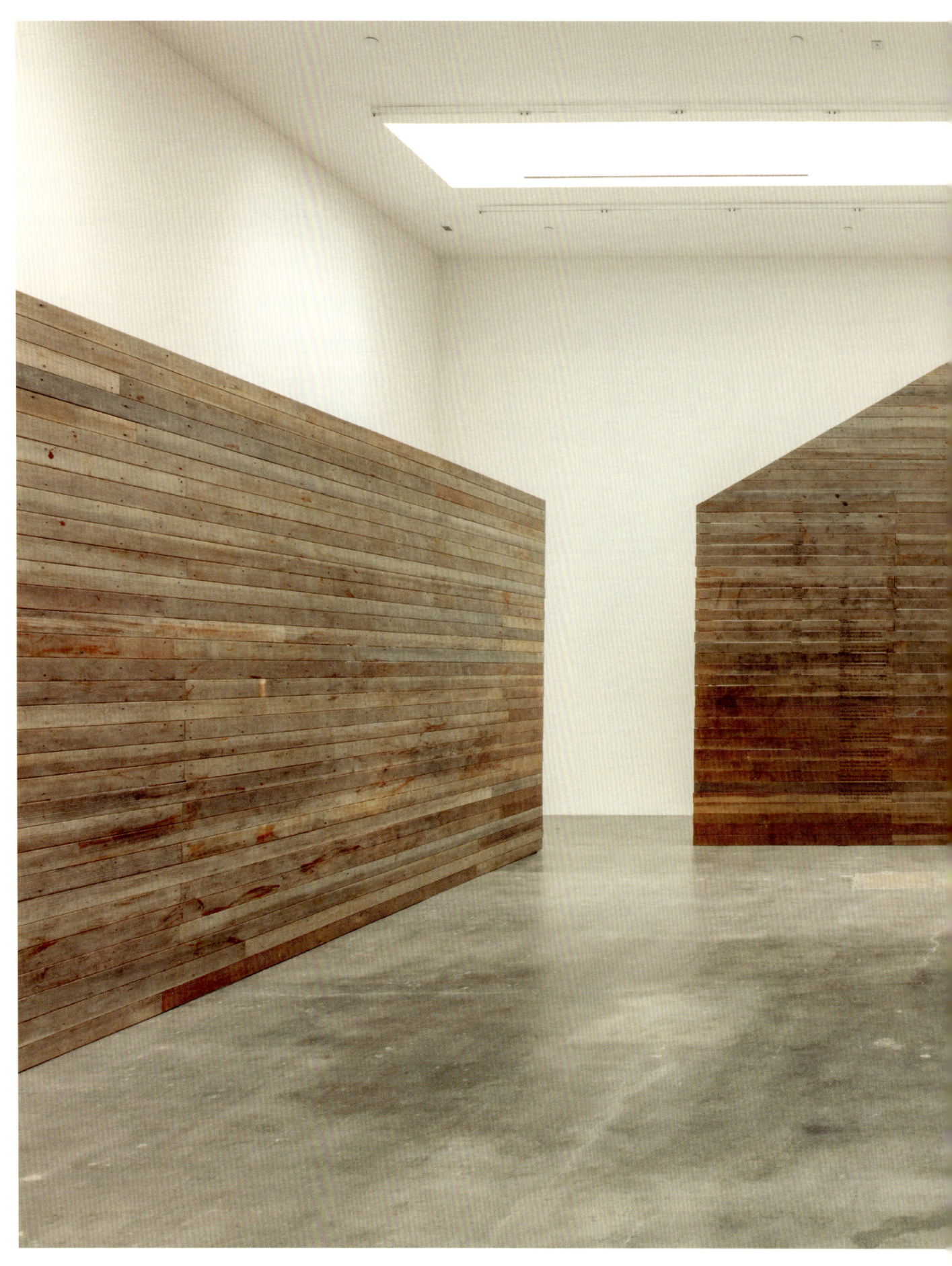

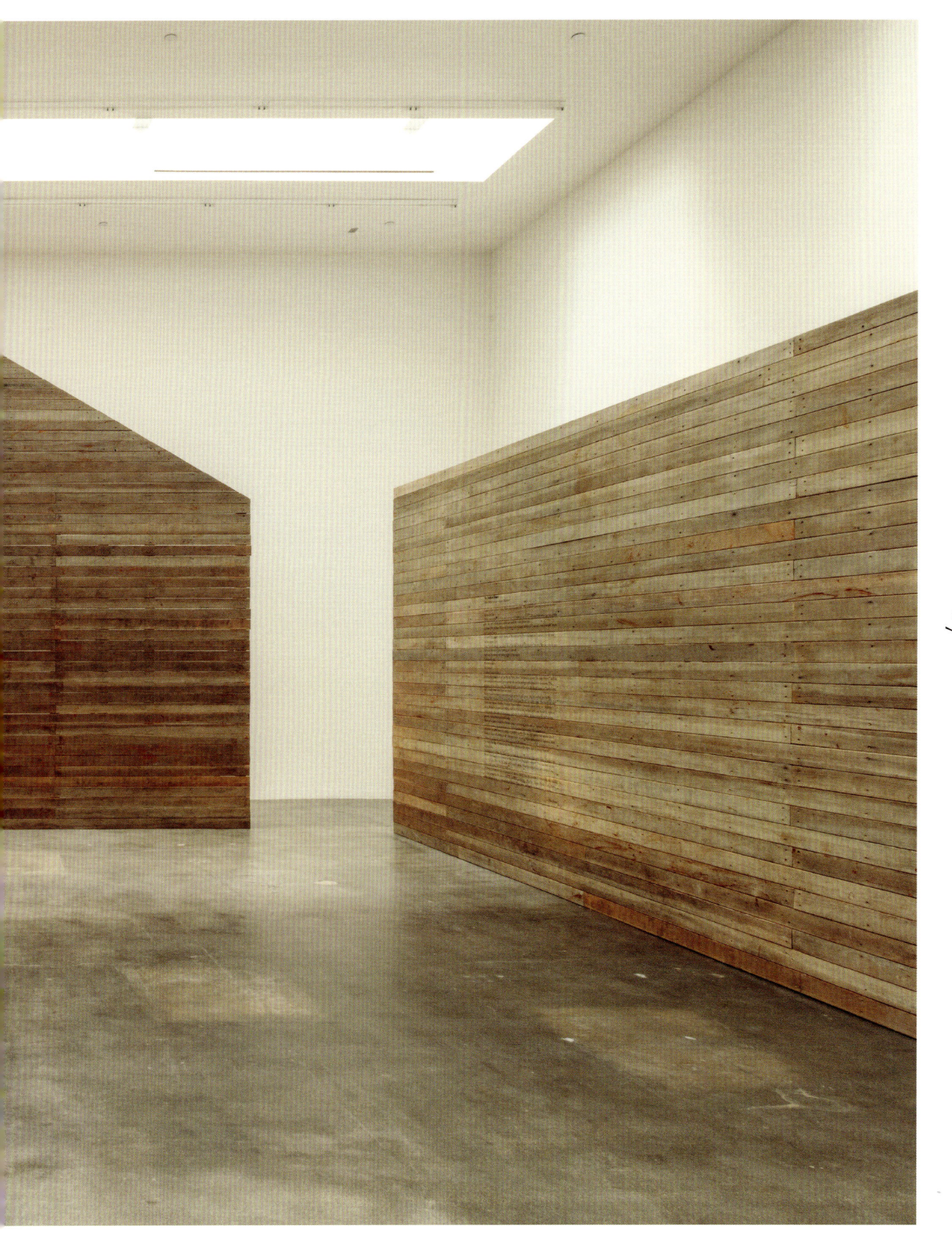

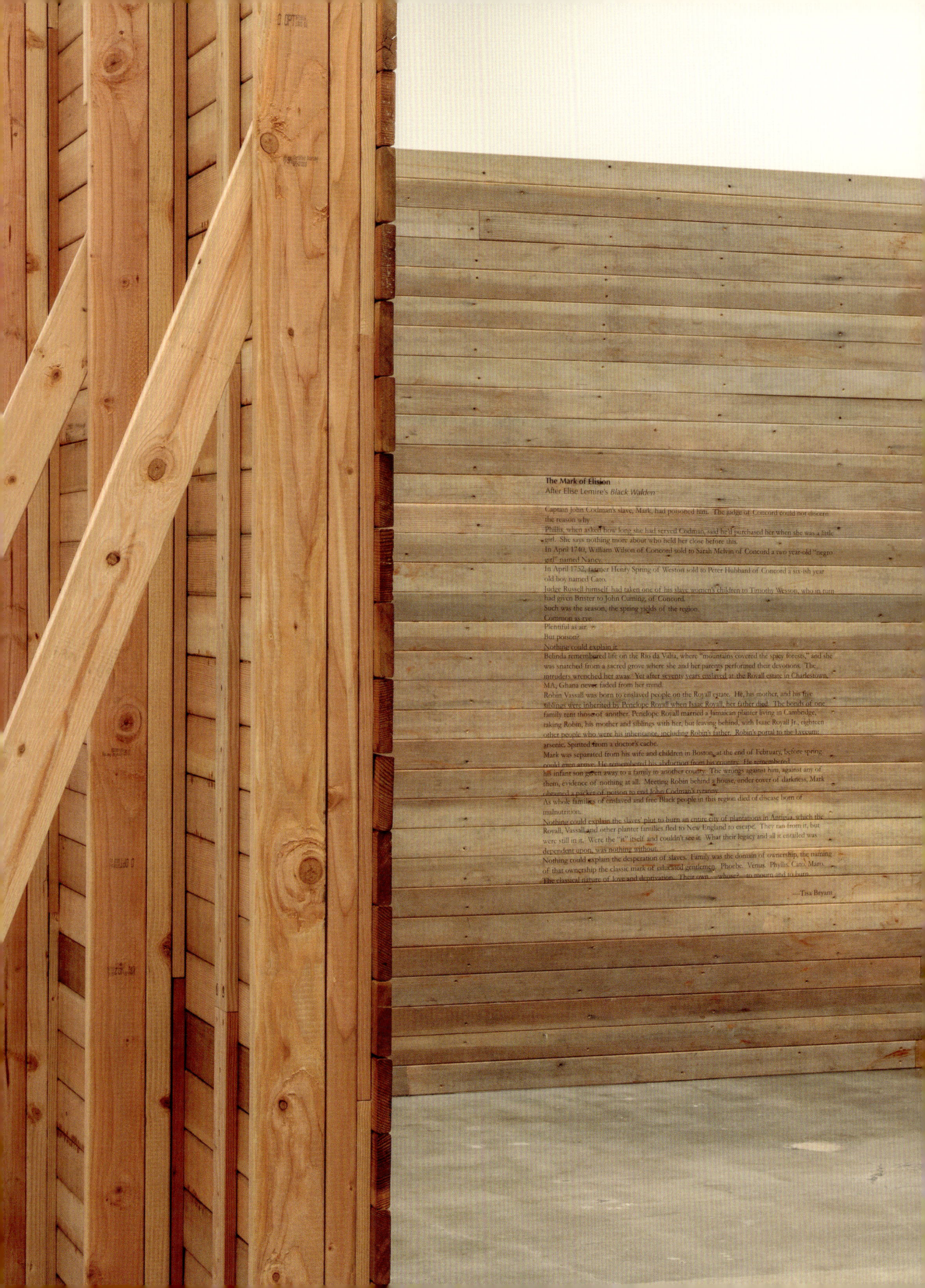

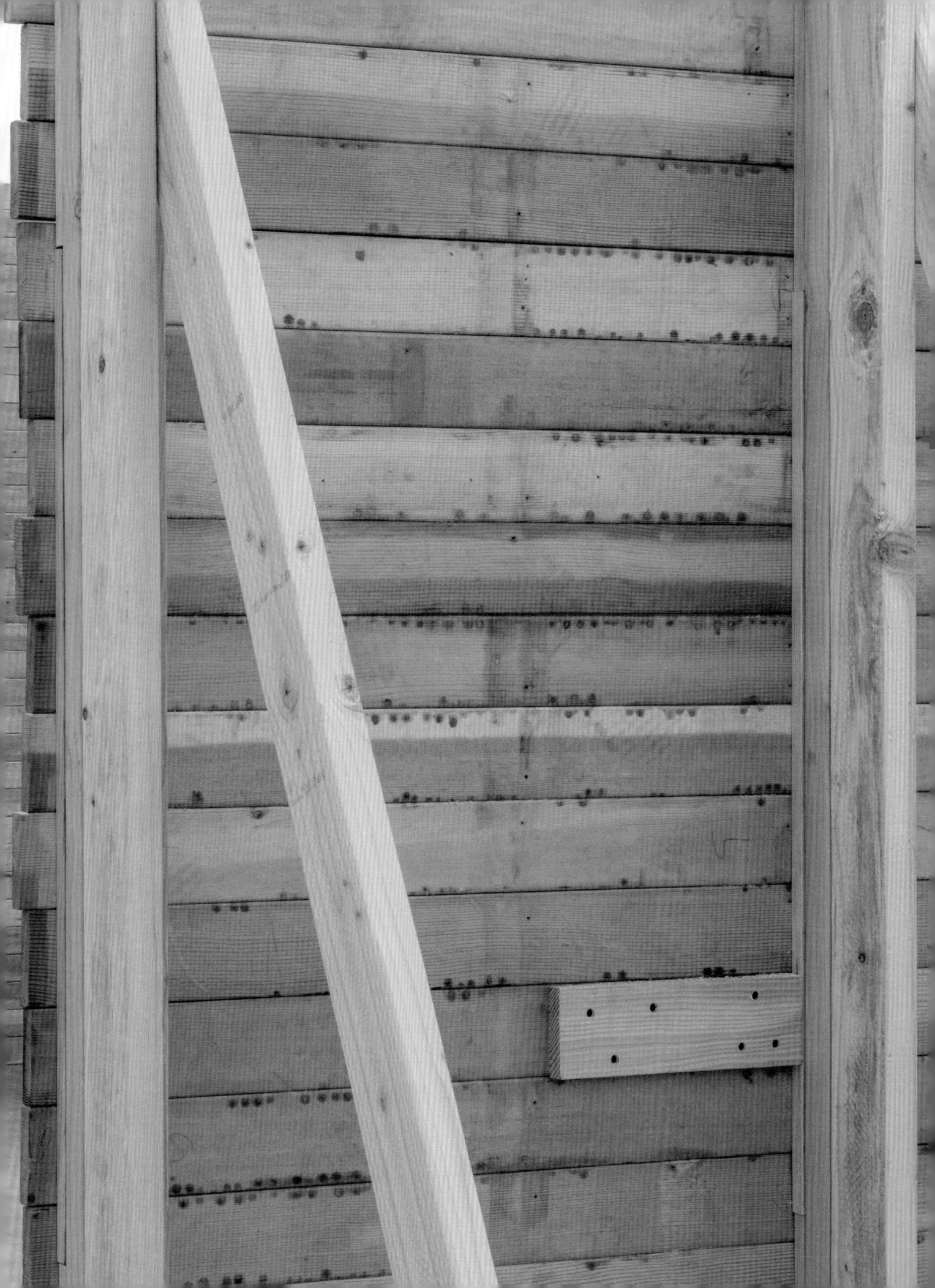

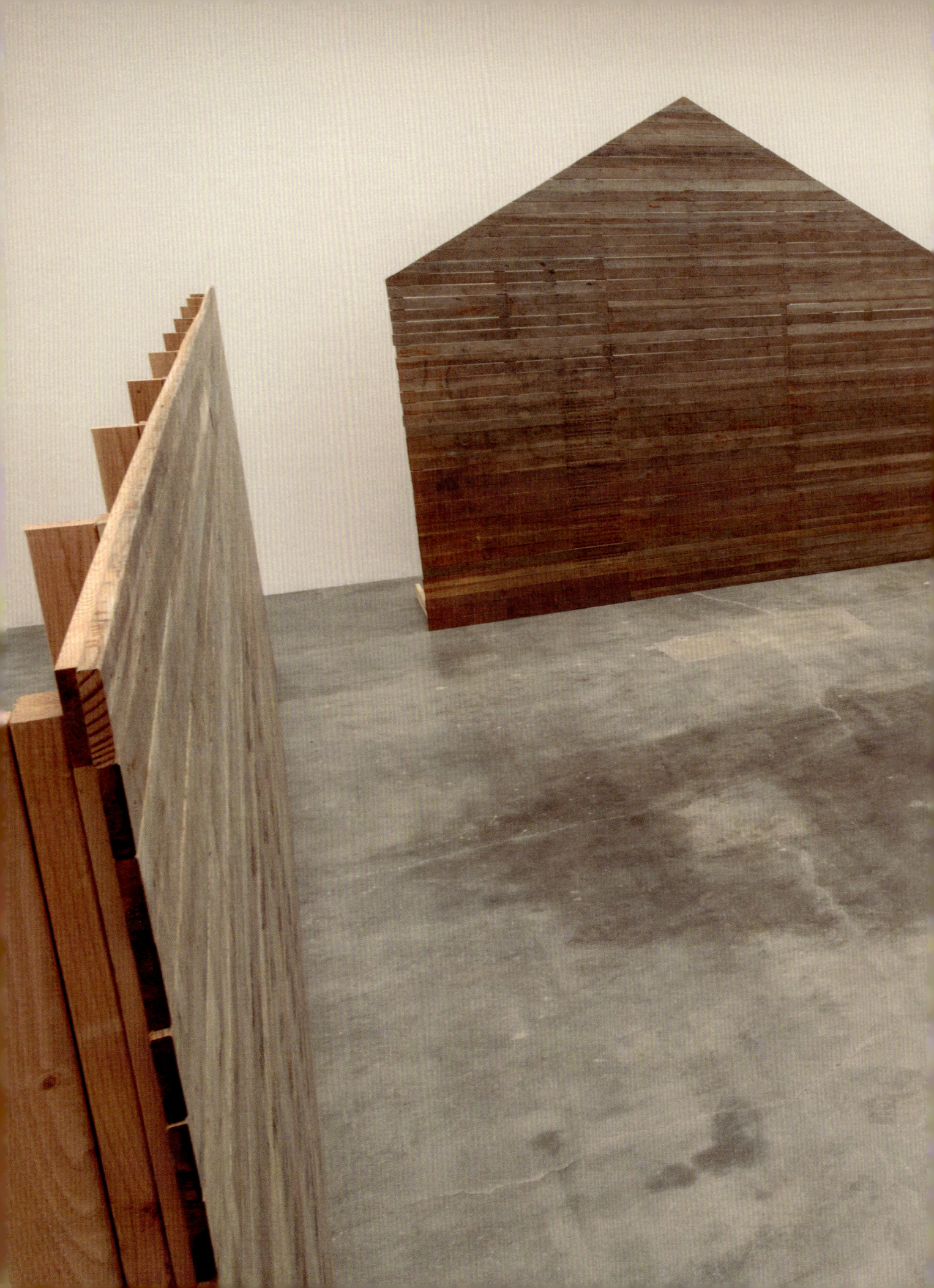

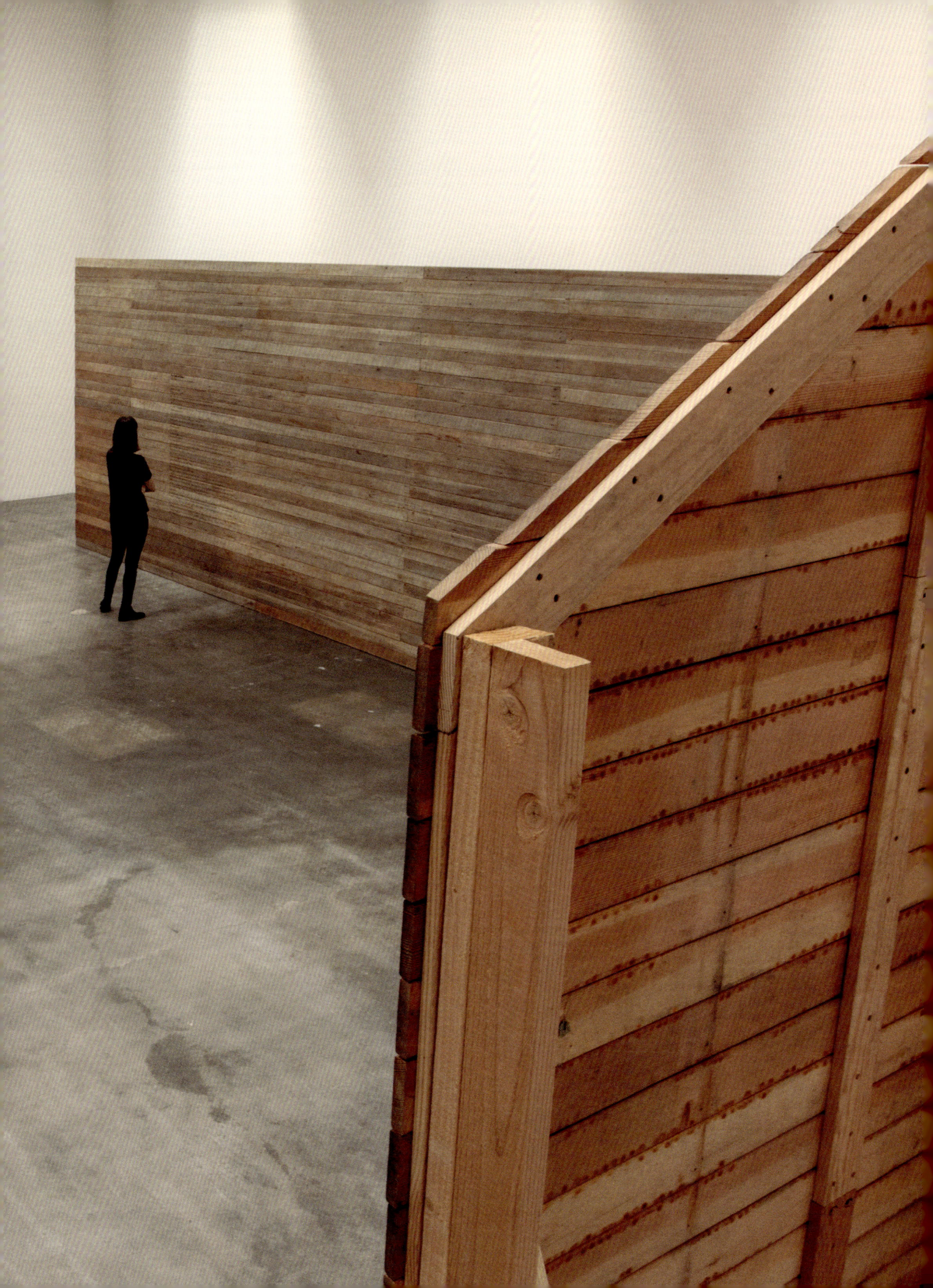

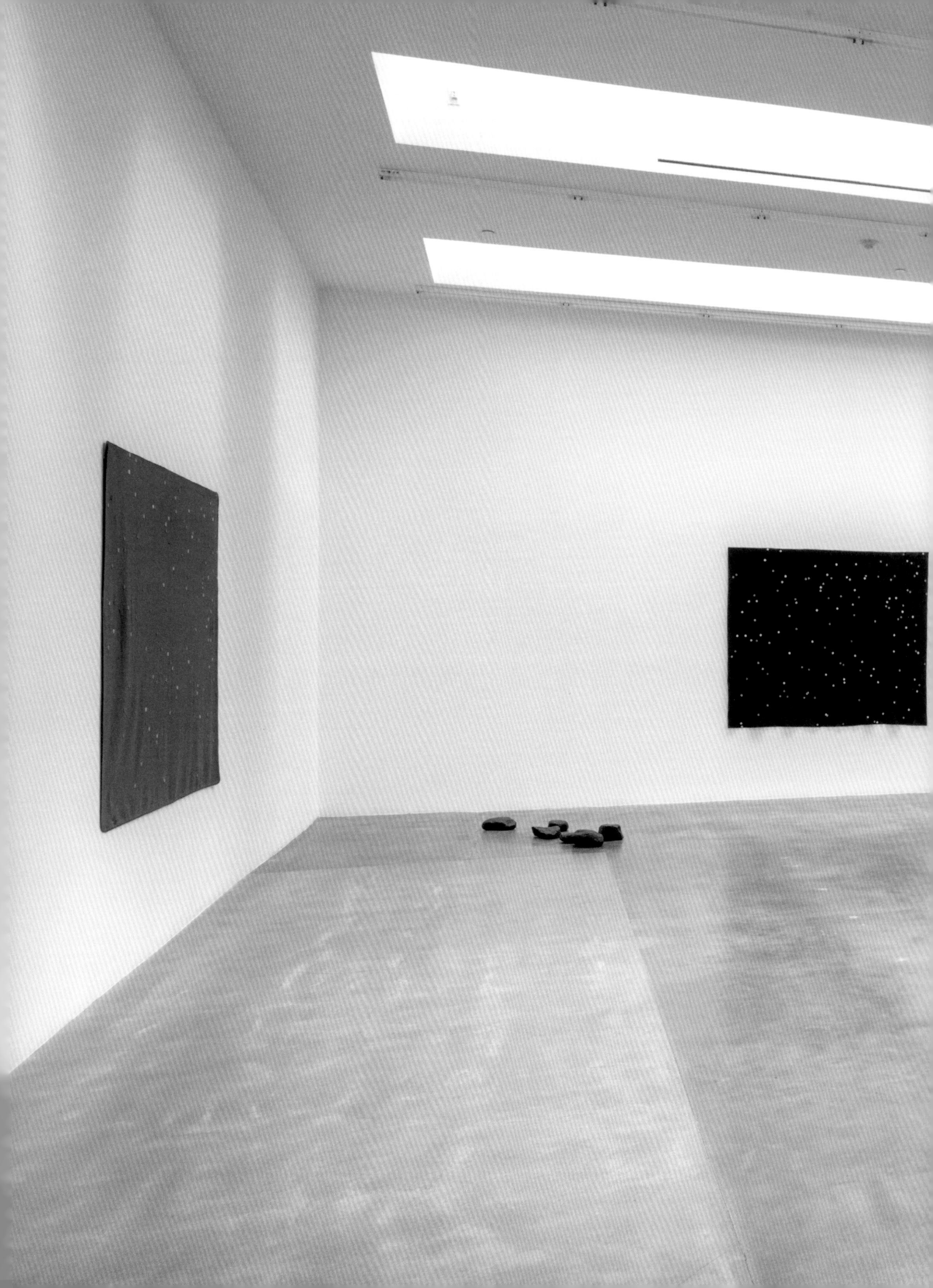

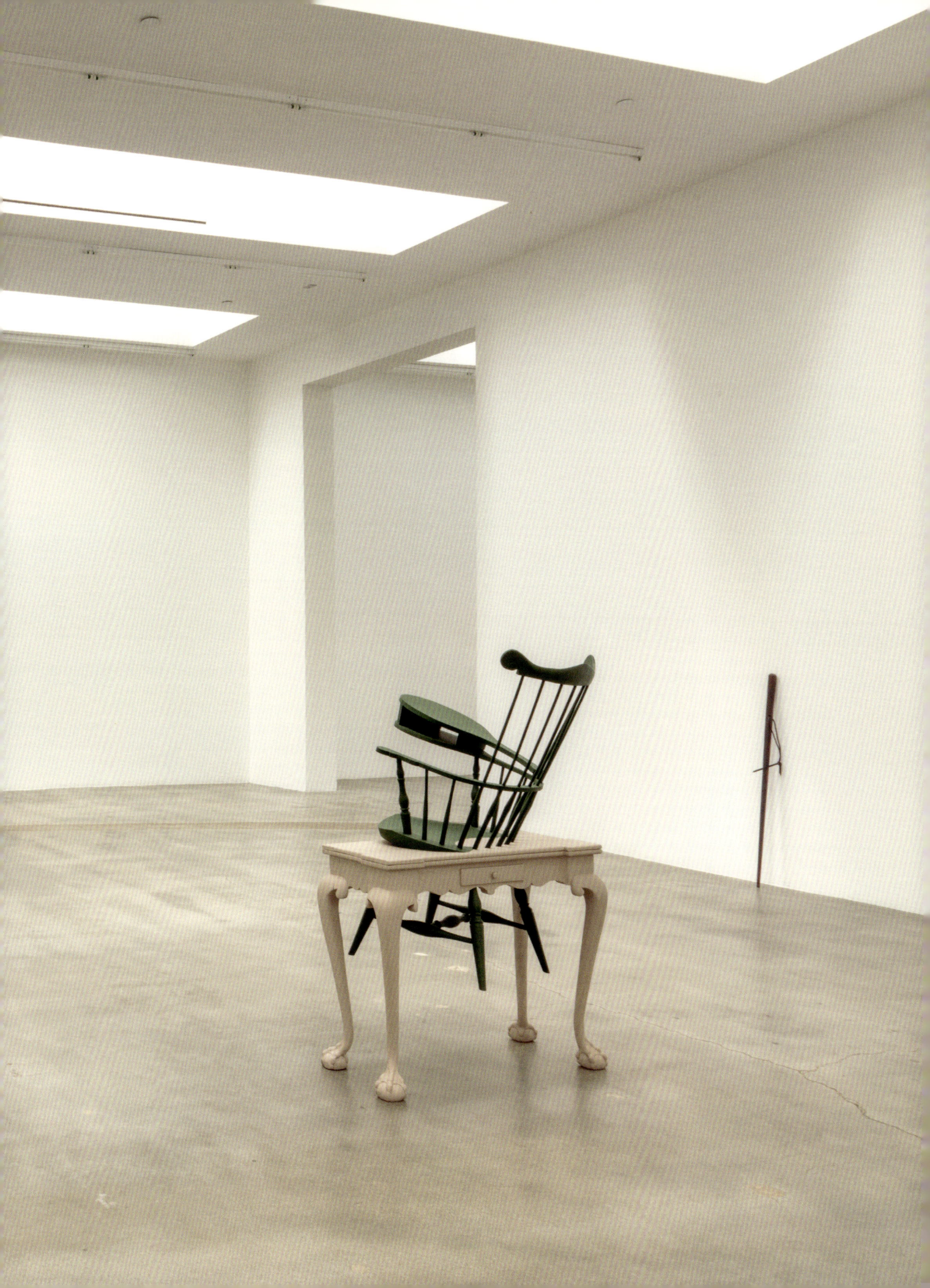

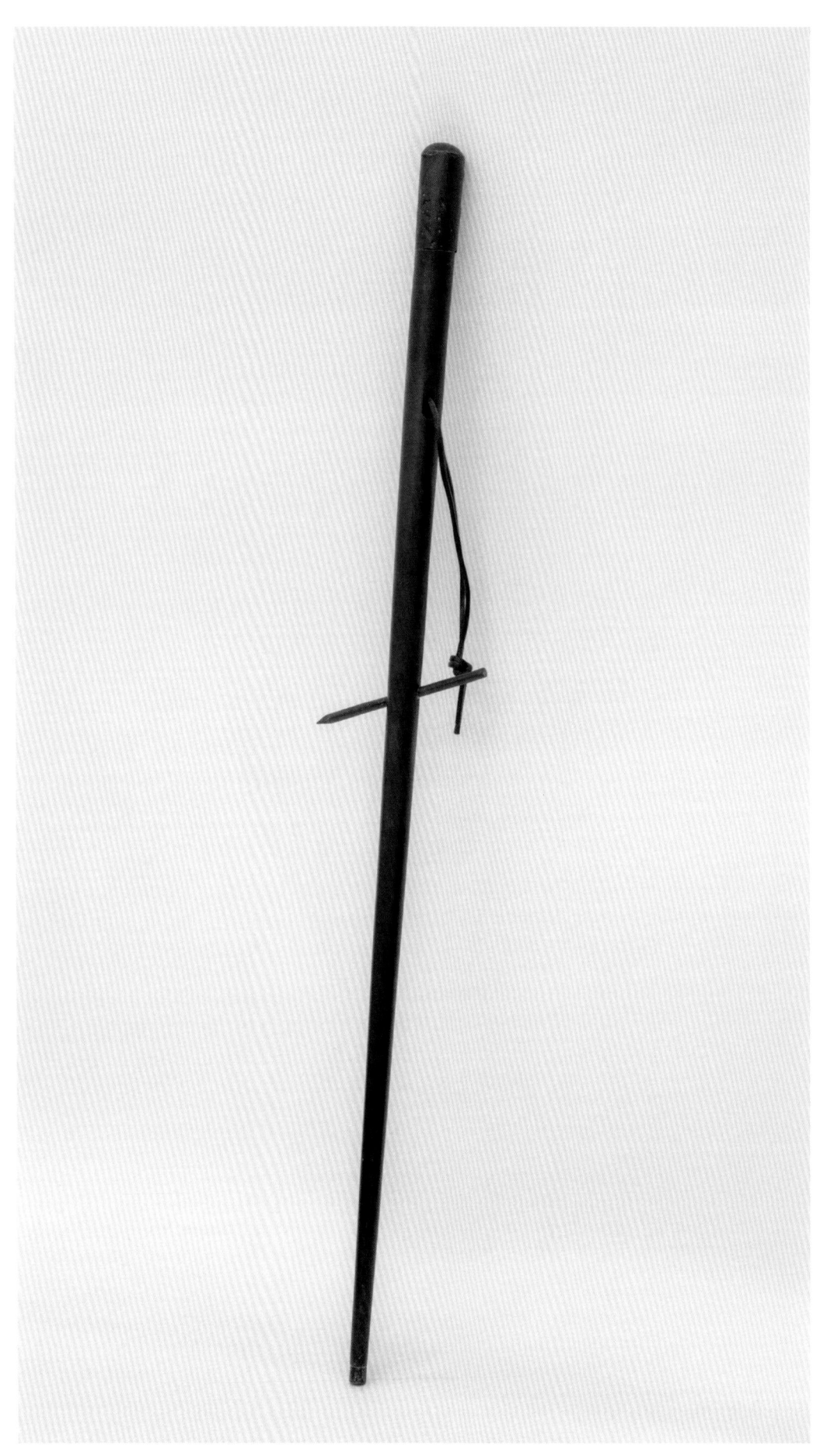

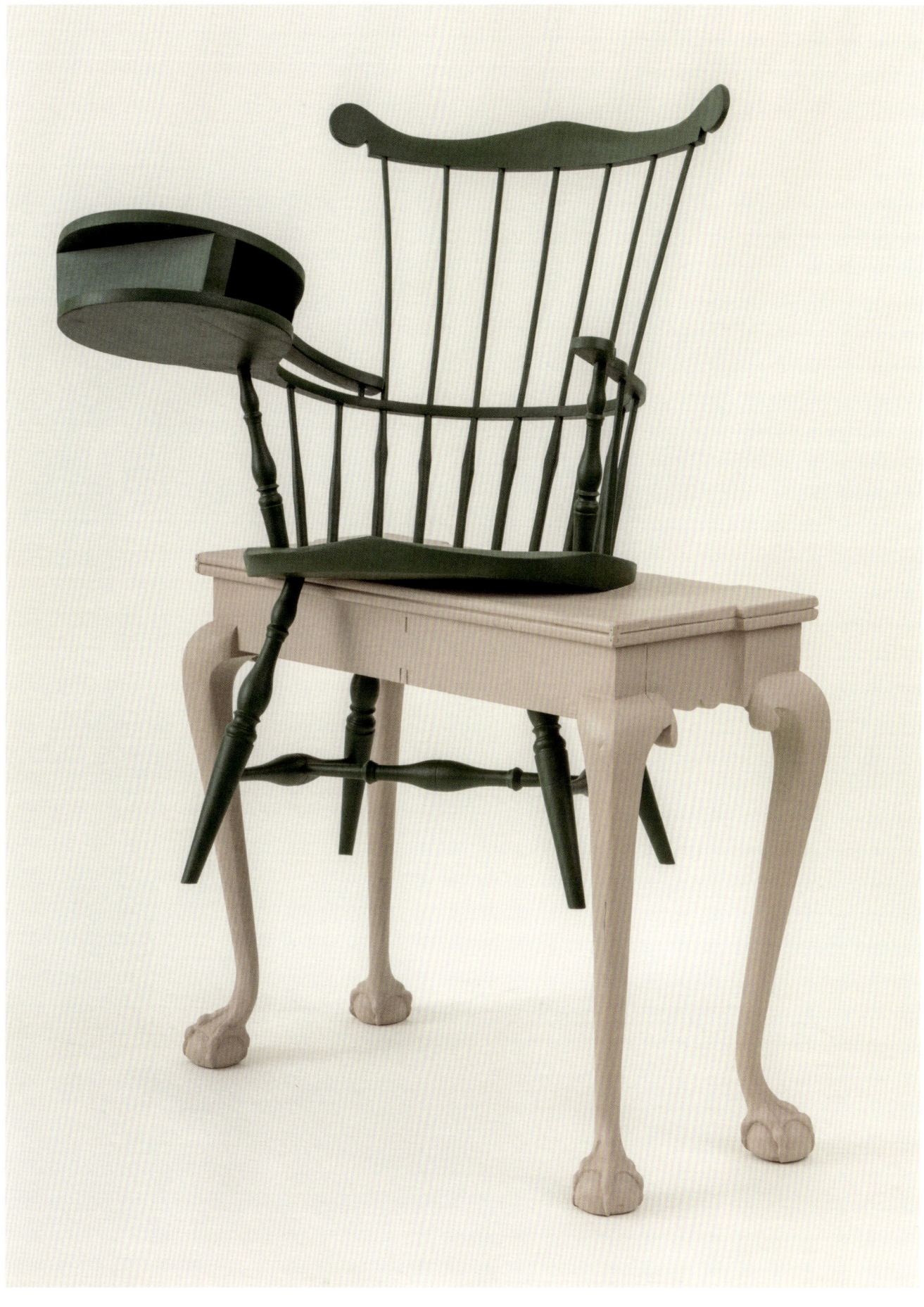

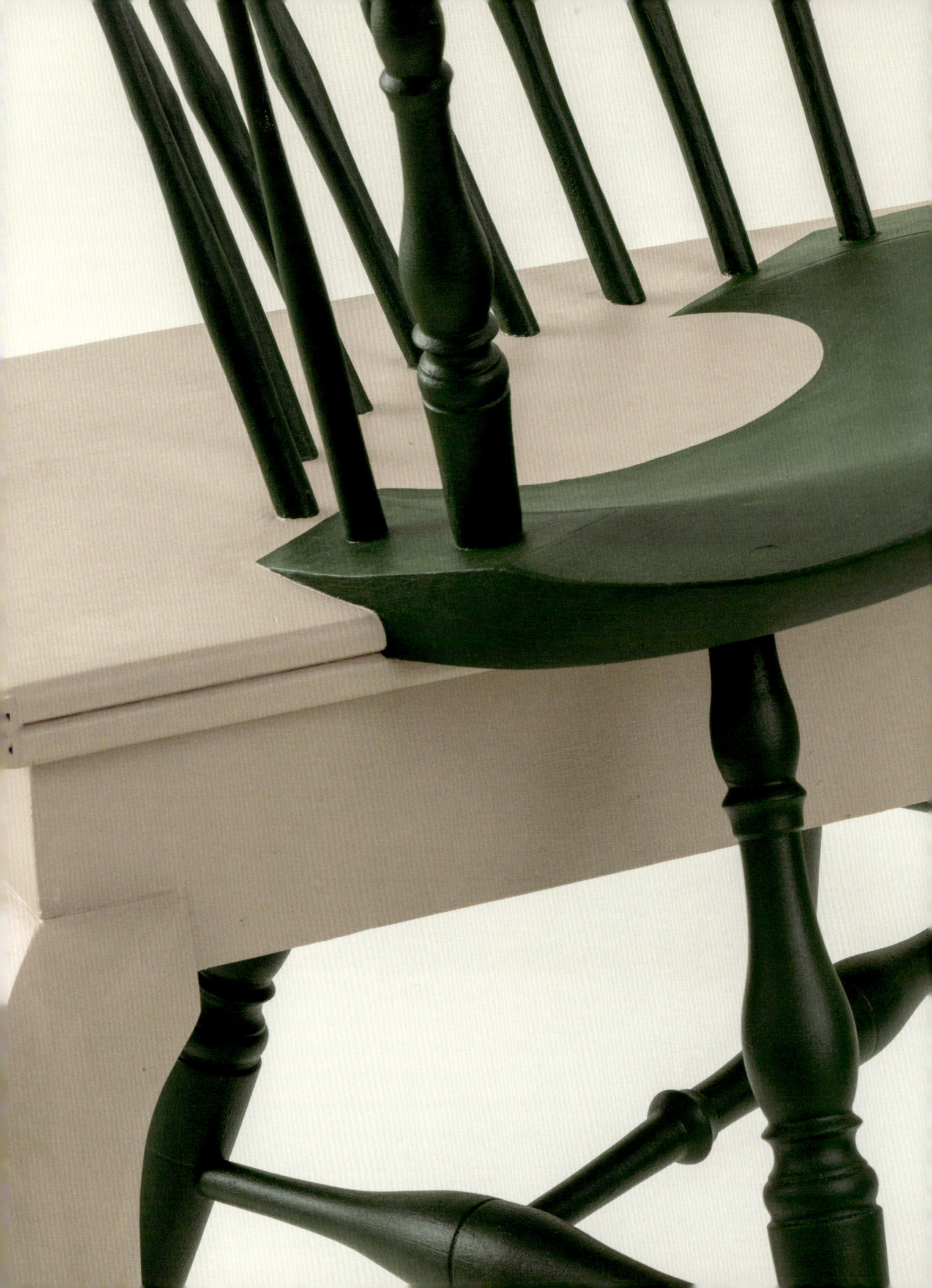

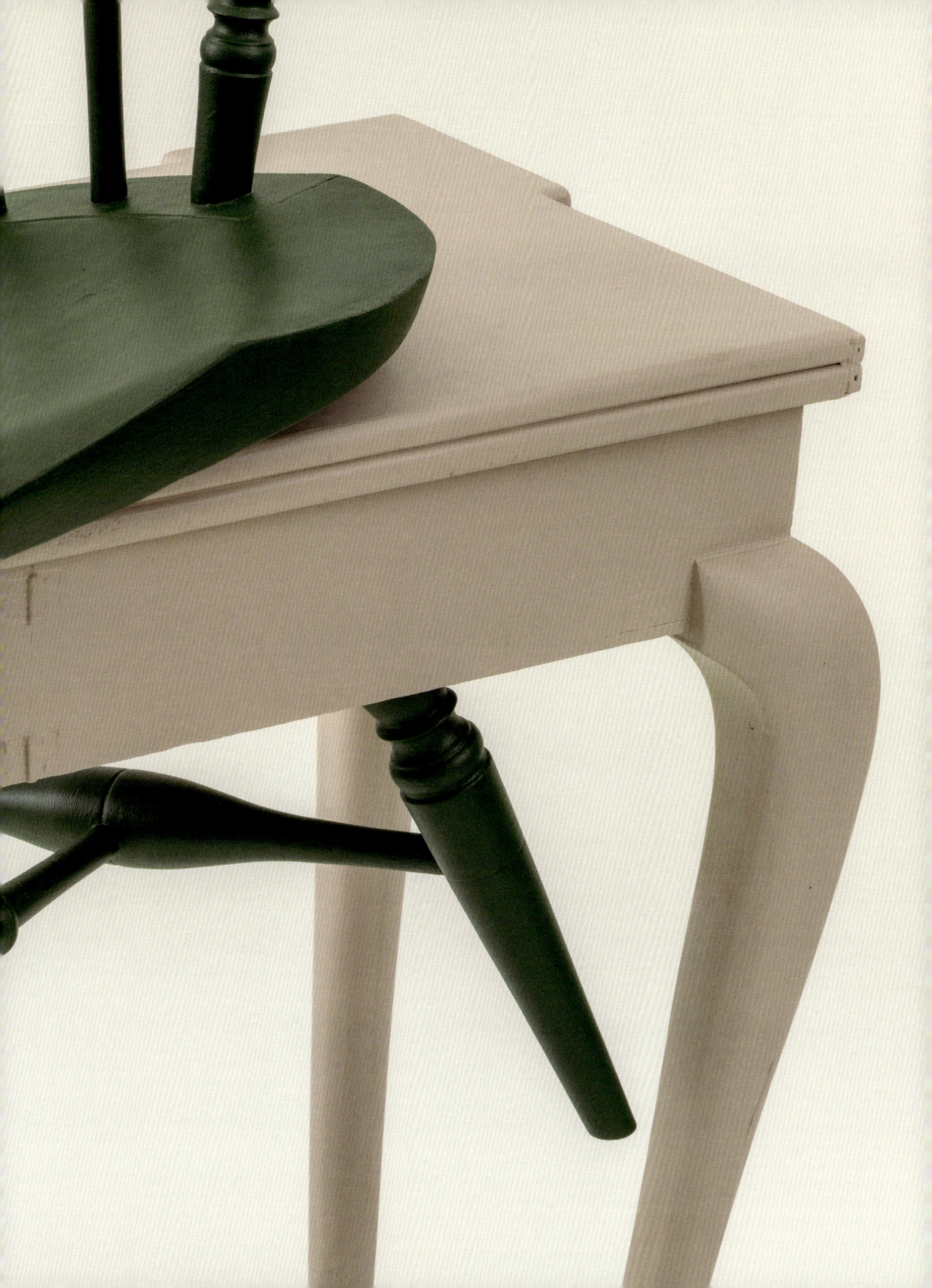

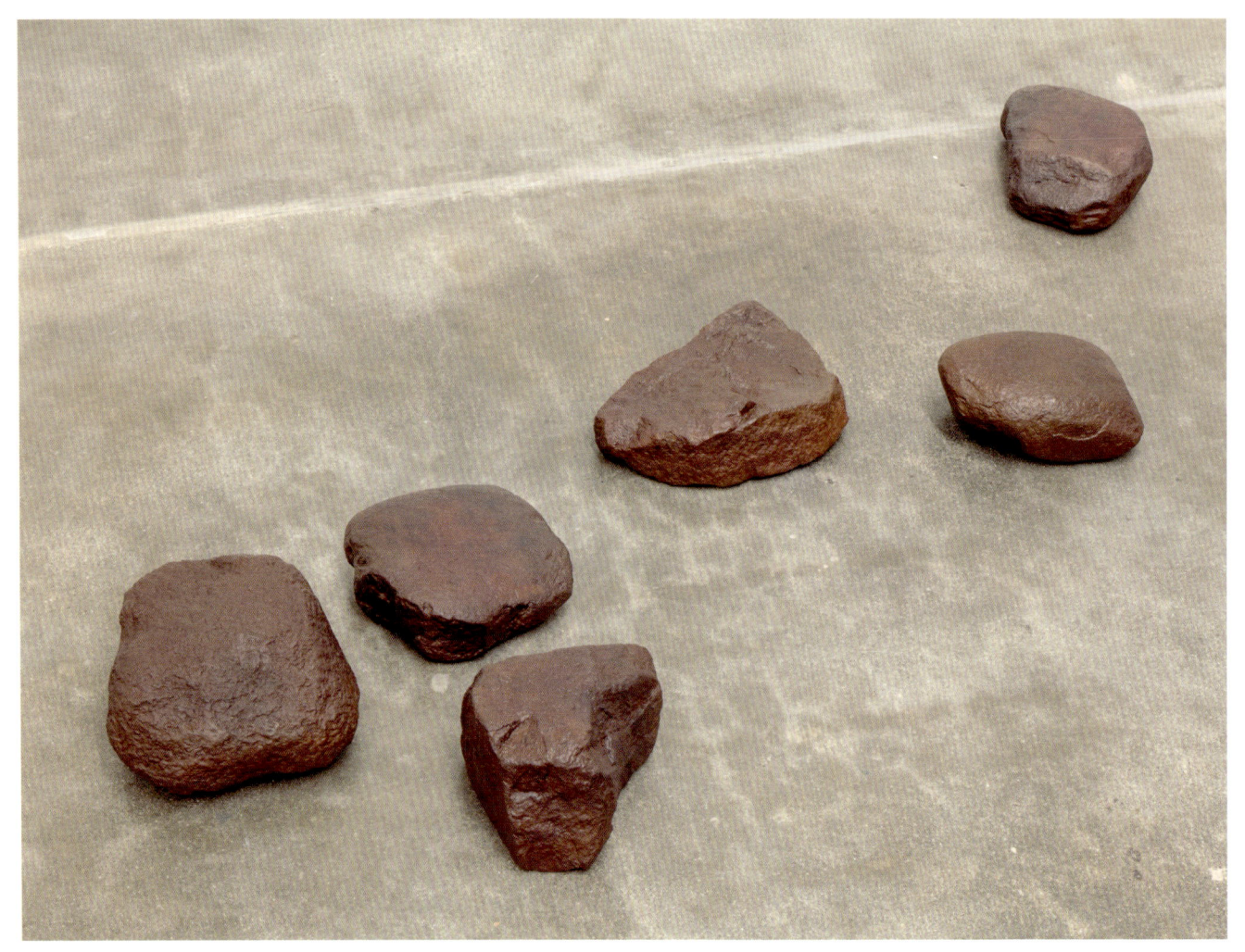

Dream Map, Ursa Minor, 2016

Dream Map, Polaris, 2016

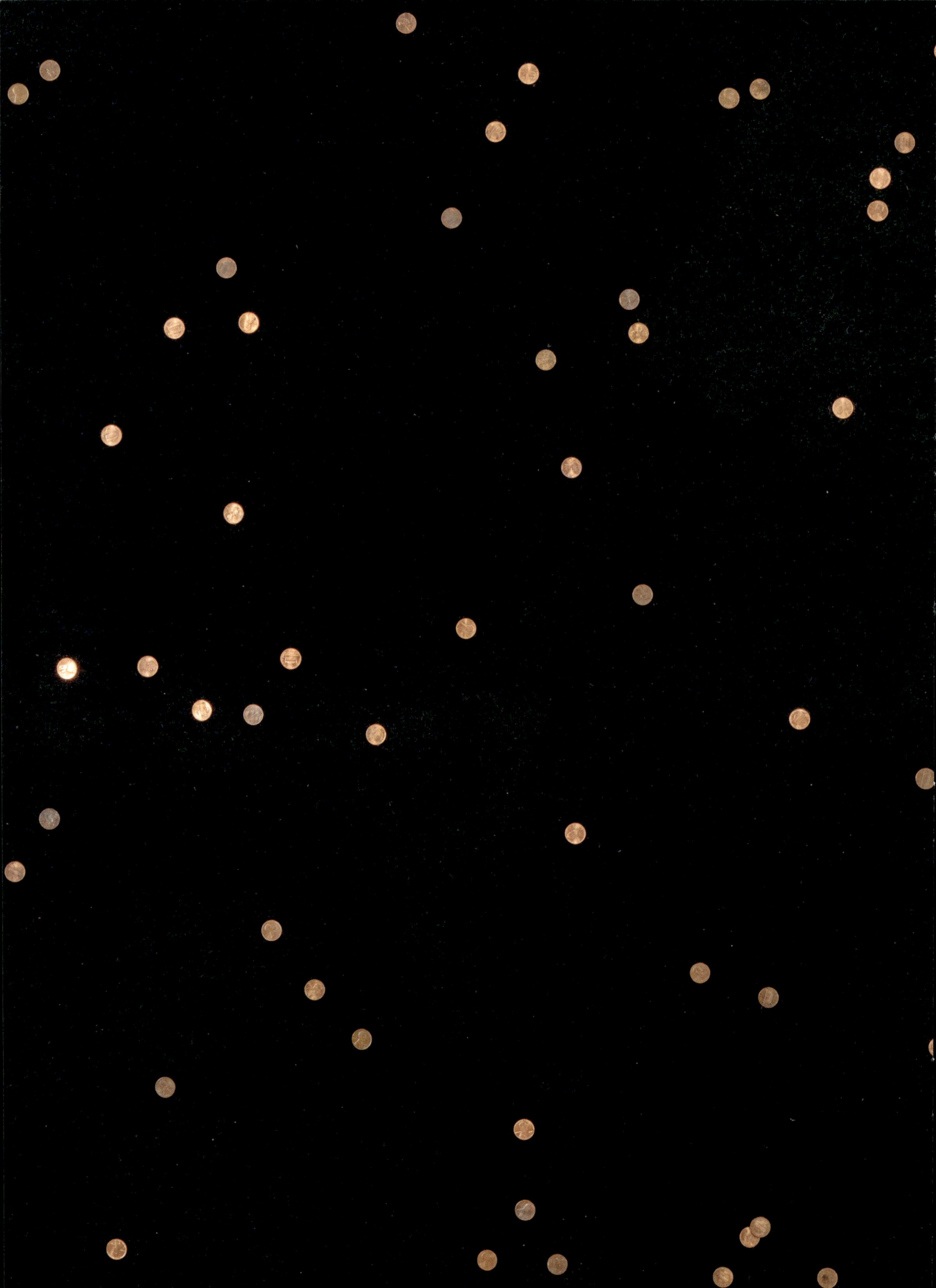

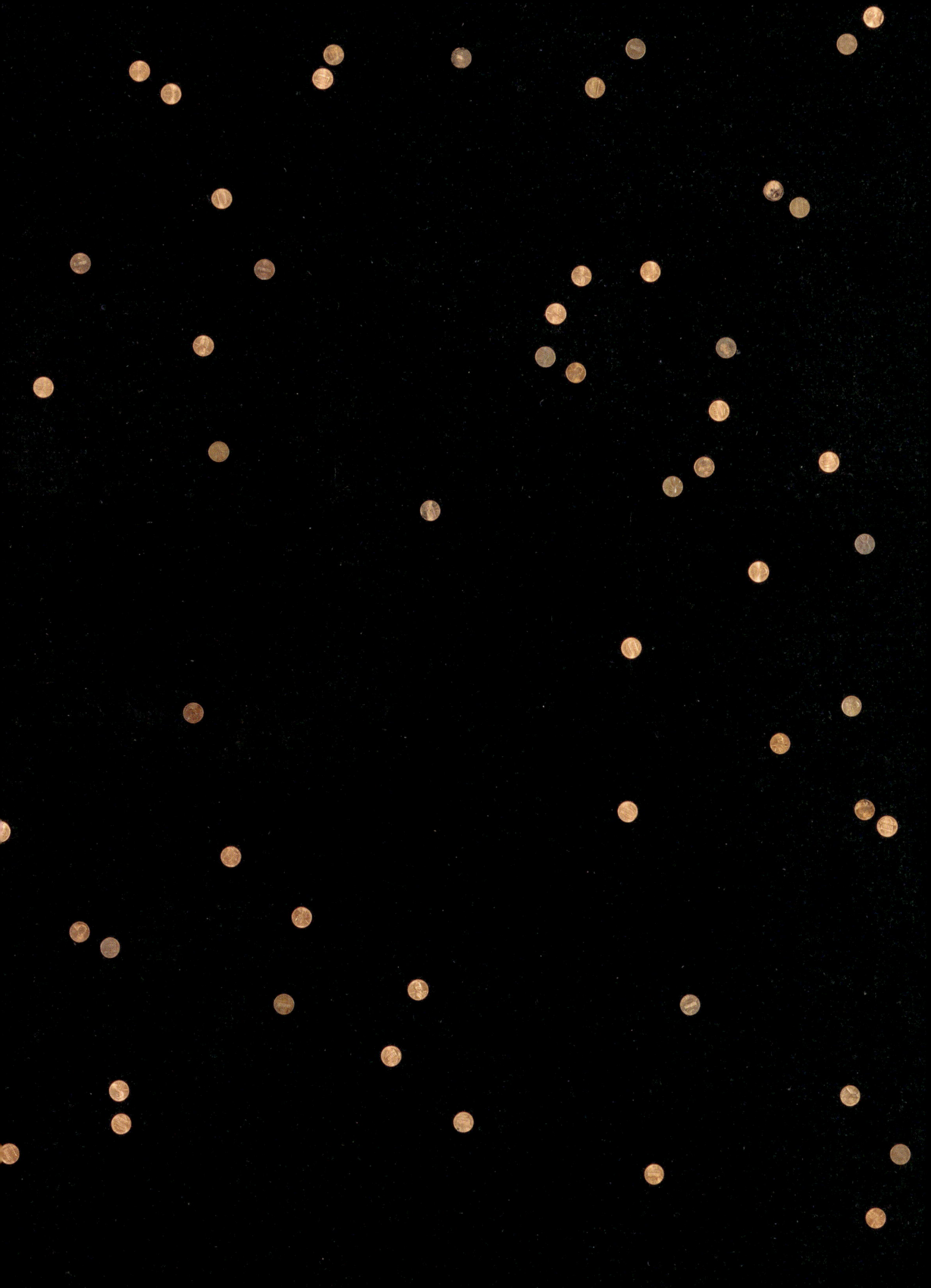

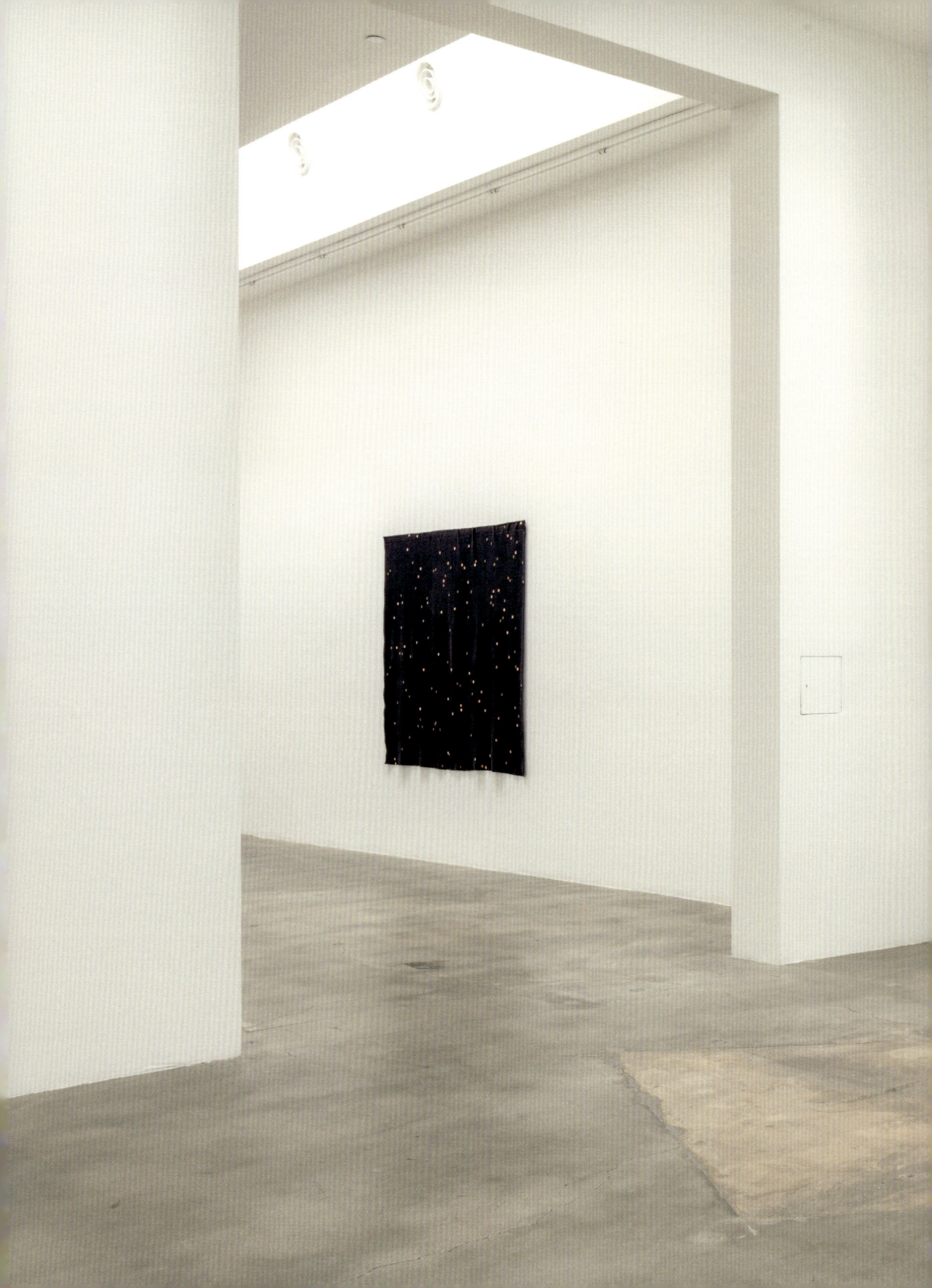

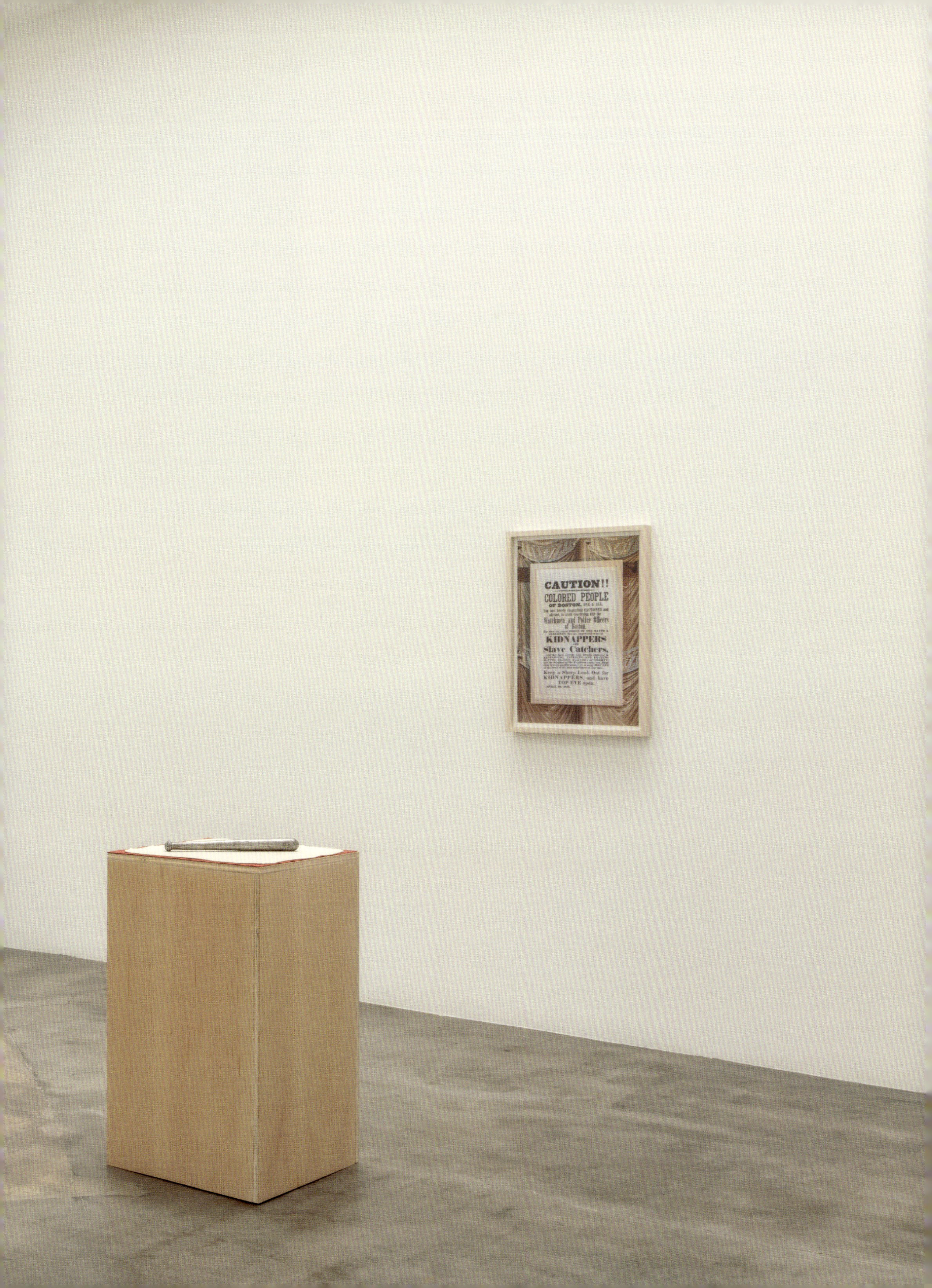

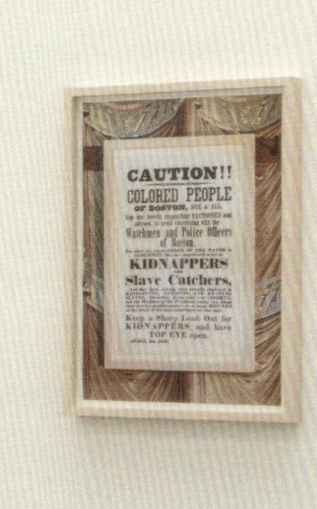

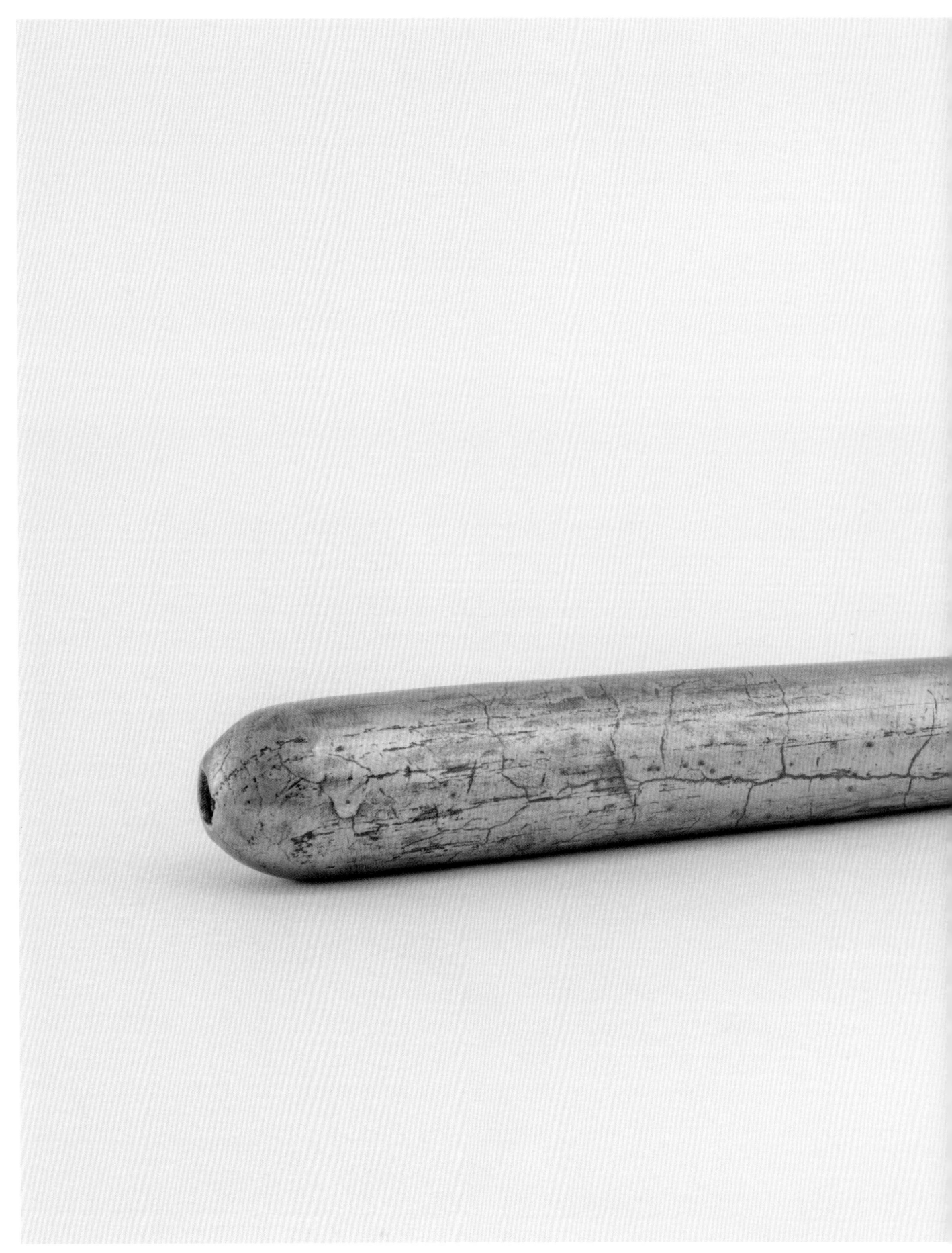

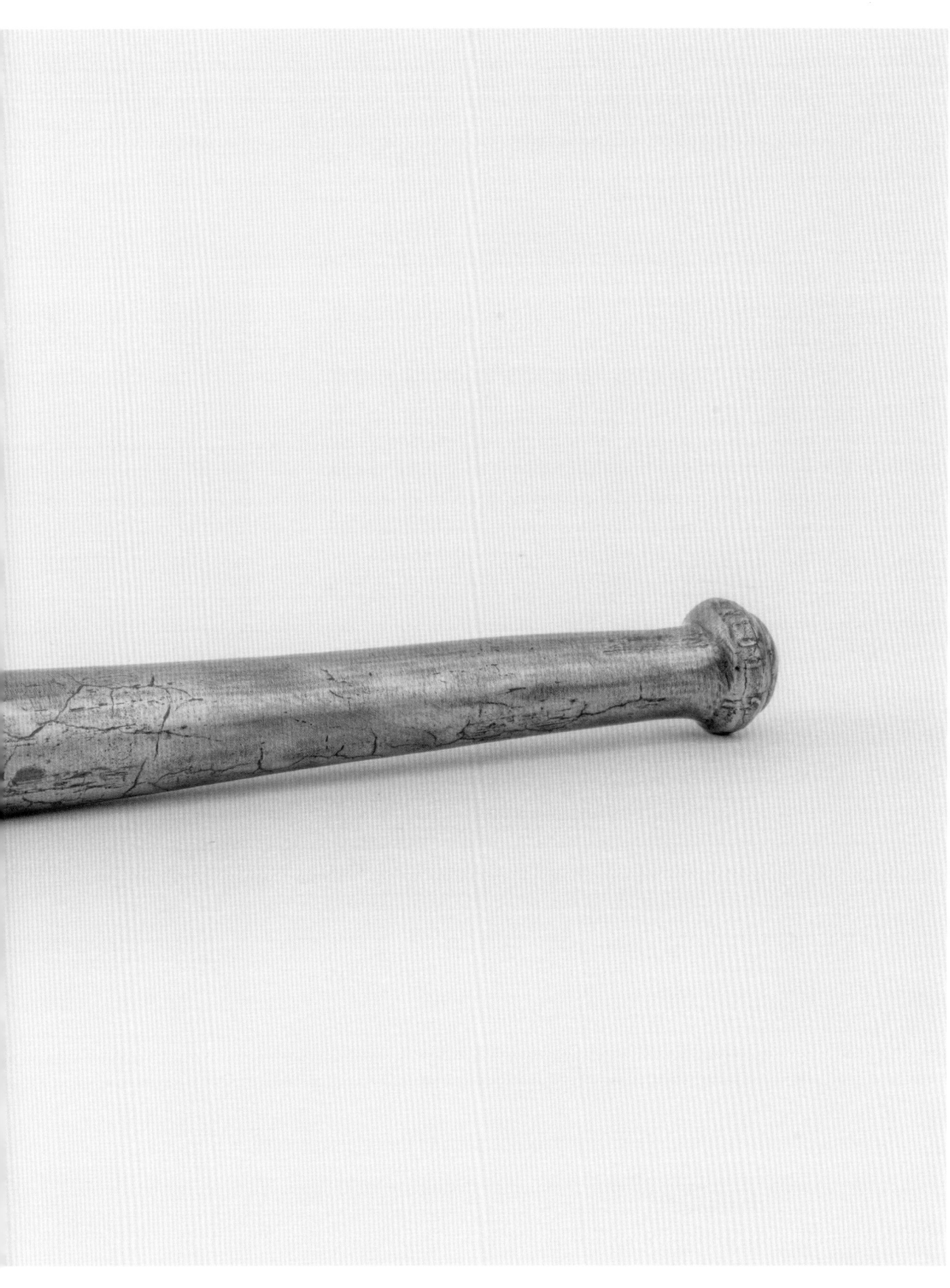

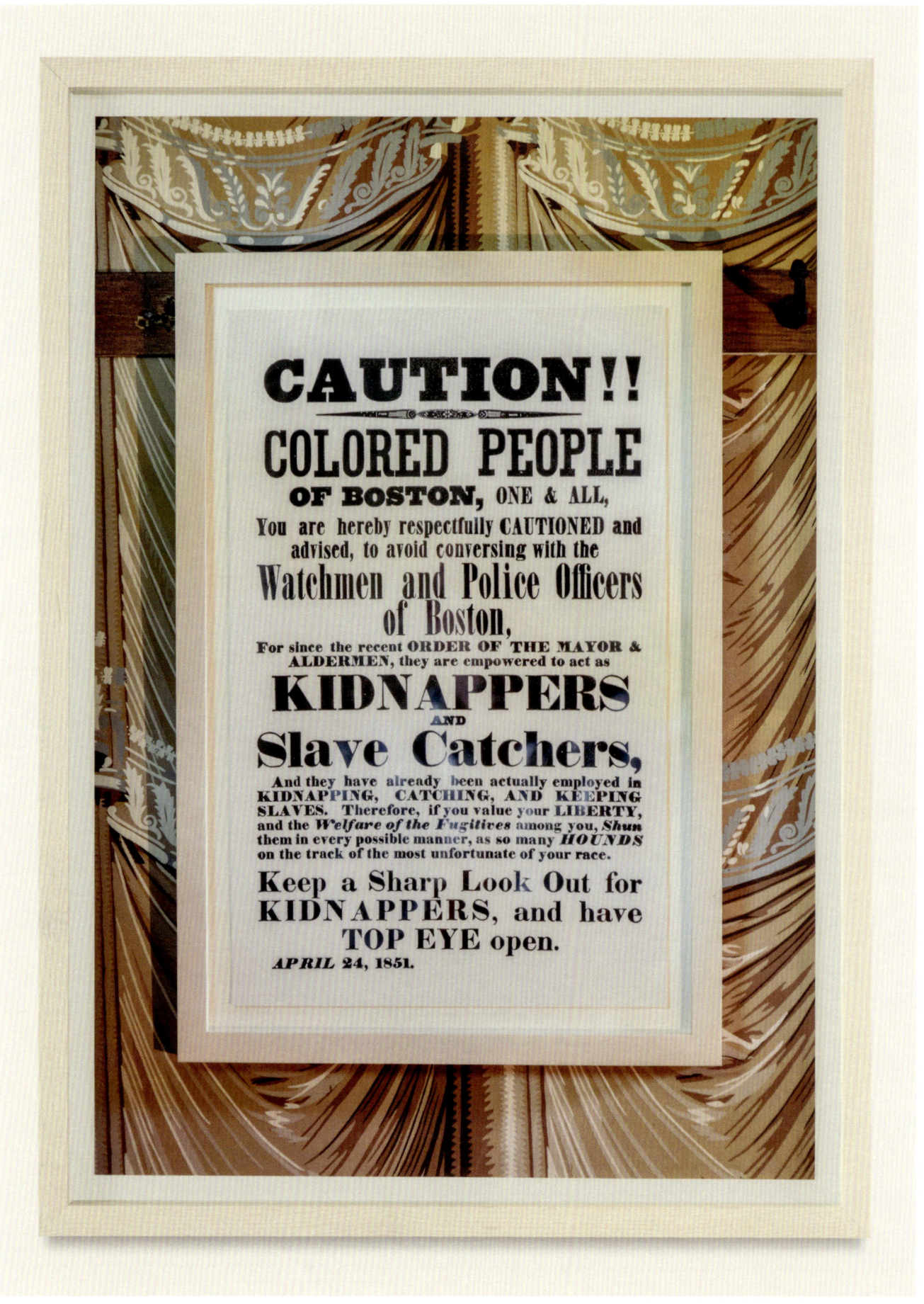

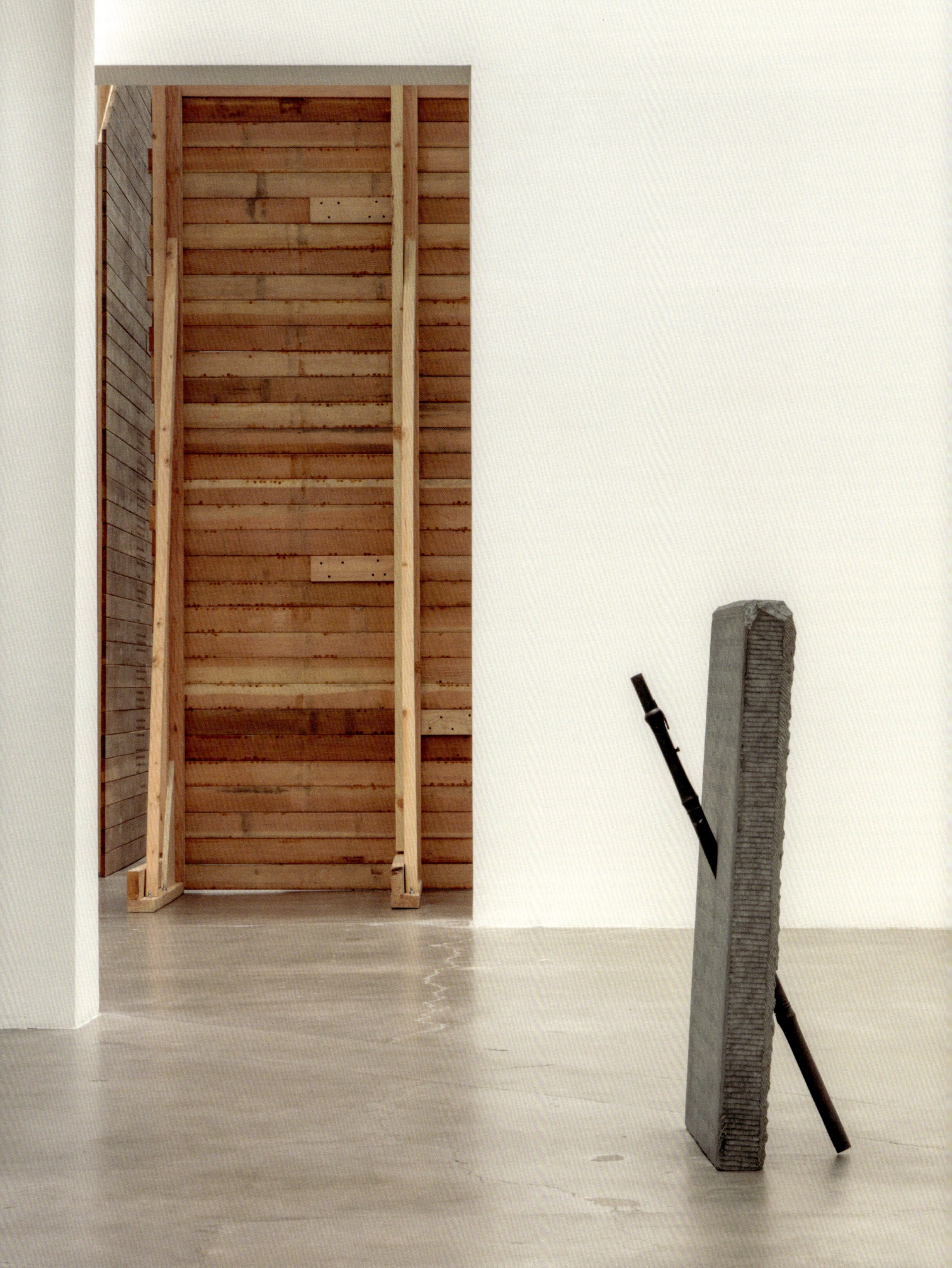

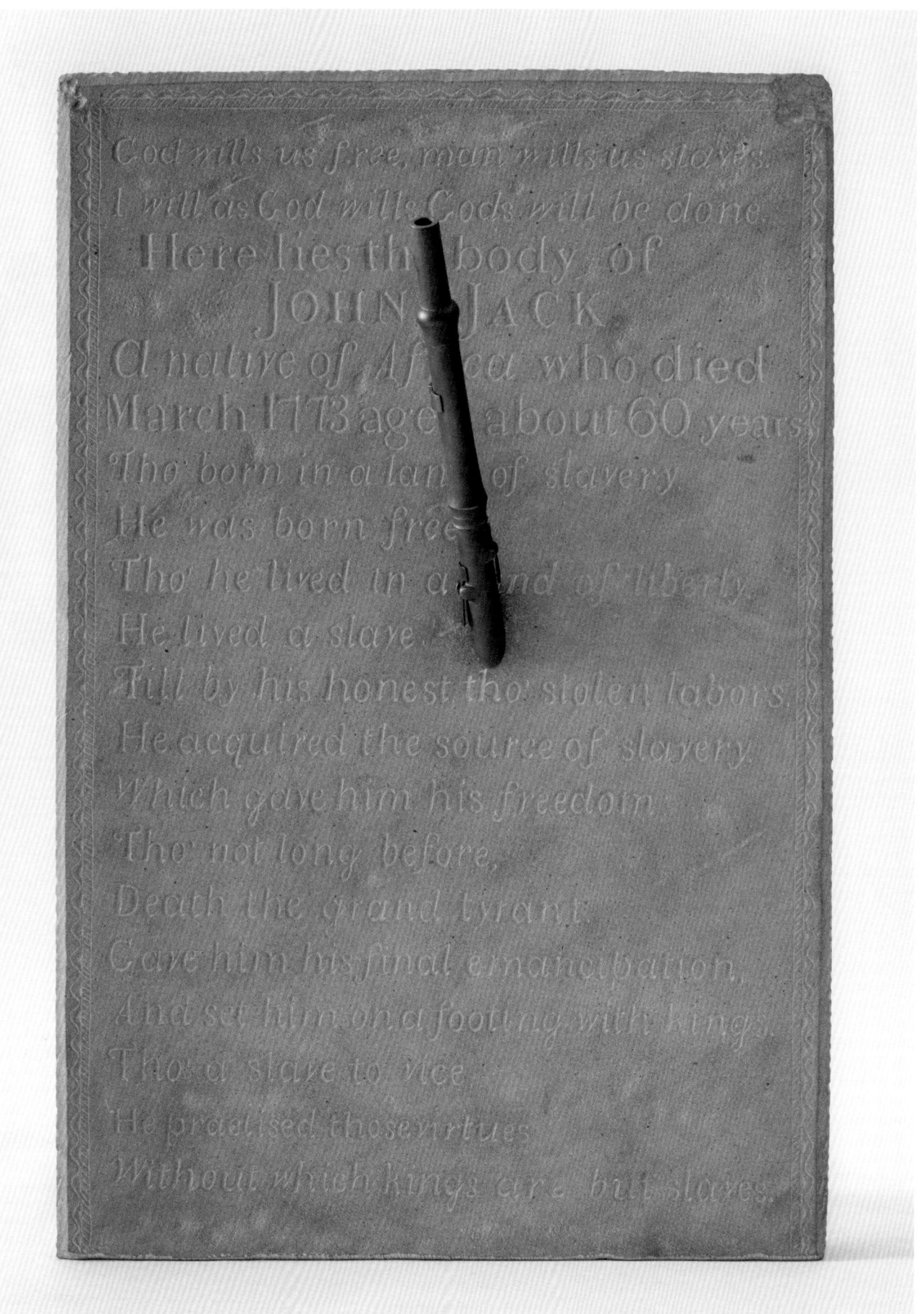

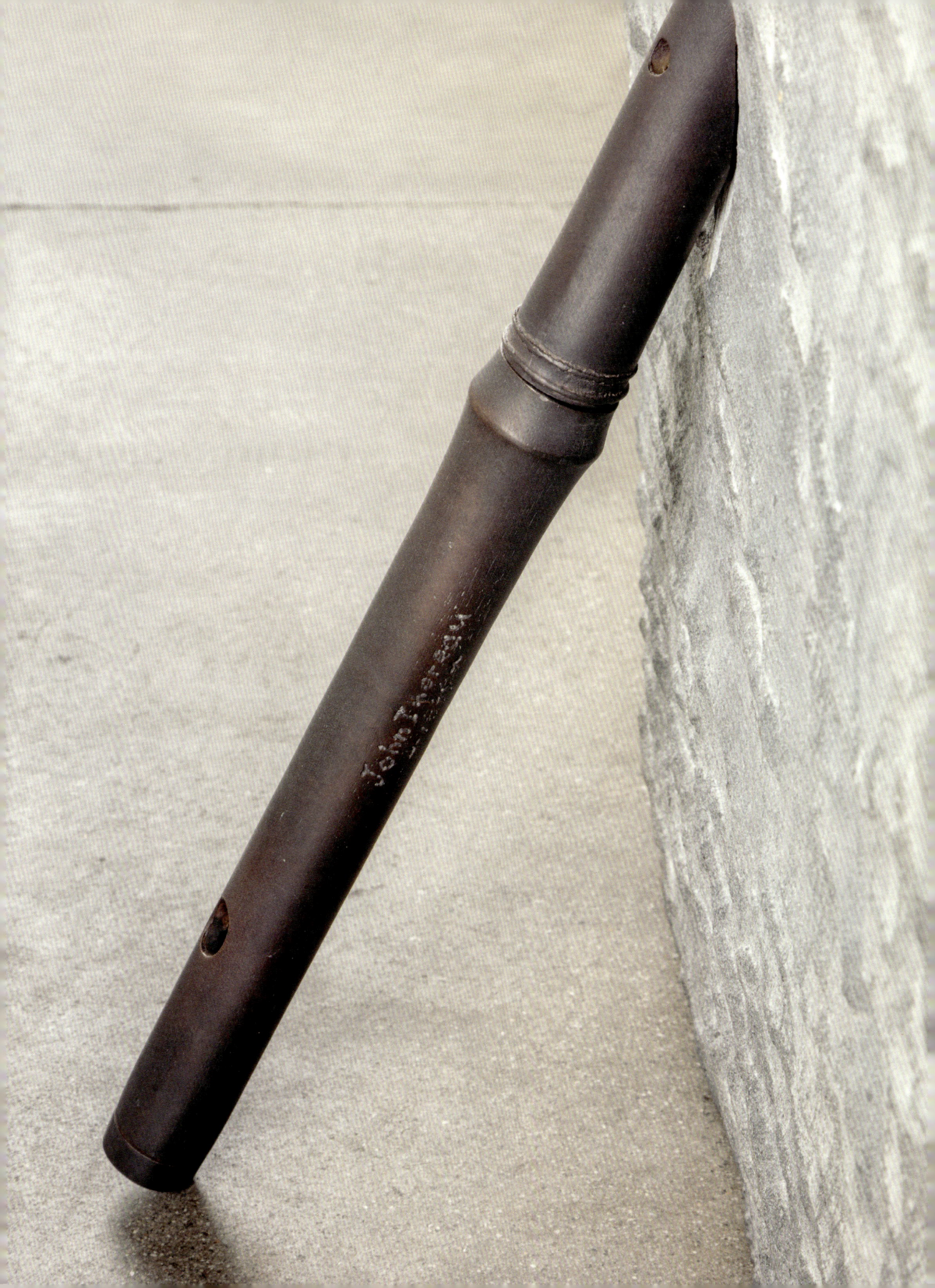

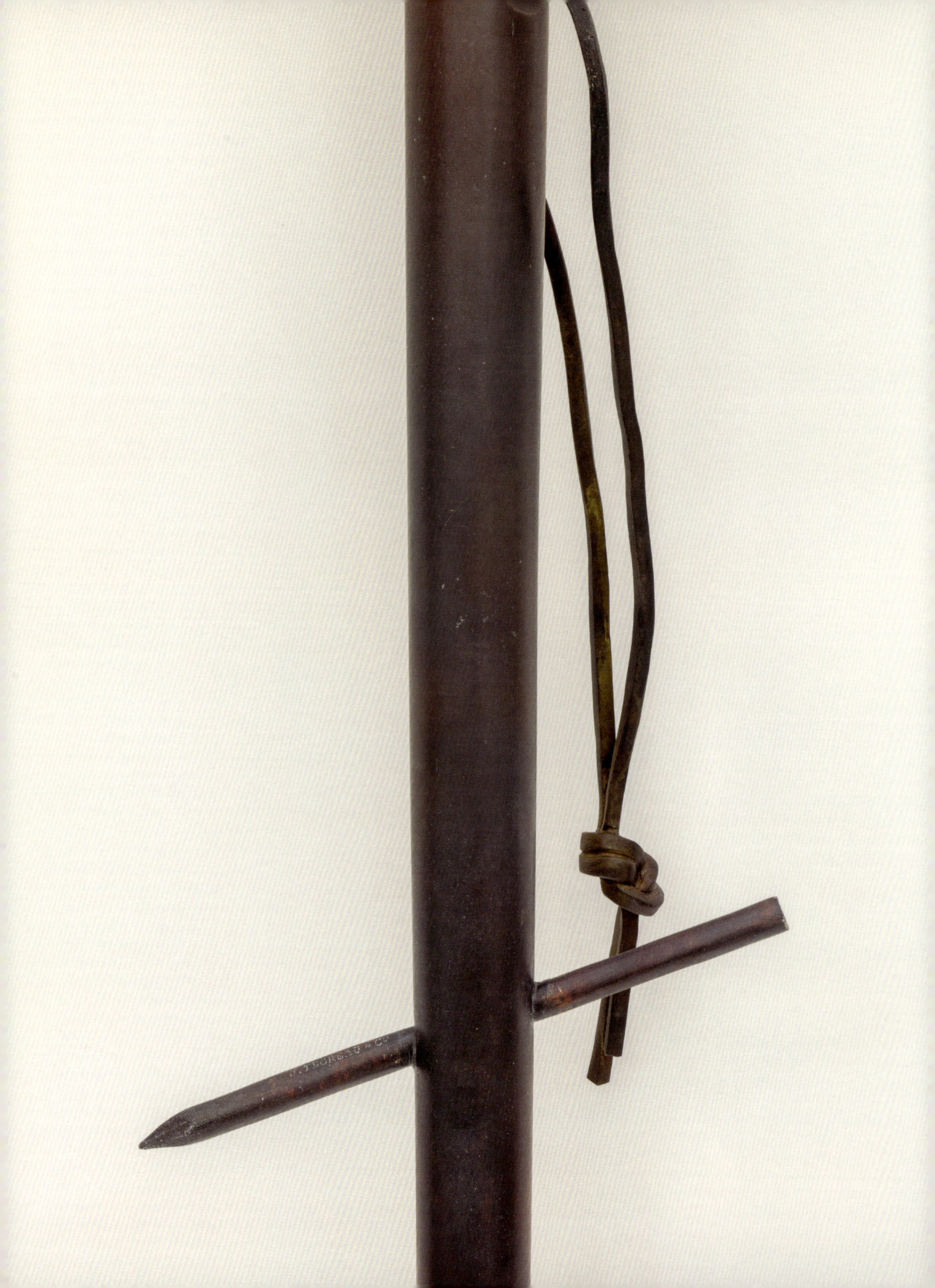

Sam Durant

Programming and Works in the Exhibitions

The Meeting House

**Curated by Pedro Alonzo,
commissioned by The Trustees**

**The Old Manse, Concord, Massachusetts
August 13–October 31, 2016**

The Meeting House, 2016
Wood, fabric pavilion, steel
Approximately 408×696×216 in (1036.3×1767.84×548.6 cm)
Design: Estudio Teddy Cruz + Forman
Engineering and Construction: Armando Plata

The Meeting House Lyceums

Lyceum I: The Picnic
August 13, 2016
Featuring: Fulani Haynes, nurse, musician, organic farmer
and food justice activist.

Lyceum II: Poetry Reading
September 24, 2016
Featuring: The poets Tisa Bryant, Robin Coste Lewis,
Danielle Legros Georges, and Kevin Young.

Lyceum III: A New Framework for Dialogue
October 15, 2016
Featuring: Adam Foss, prosecutor and juvenile justice
reformer; Barbara Lewis, director of the William Monroe
Trotter Institute at the University of Massachusetts
Boston; Penny Outlaw, co-president of Royall House &
Slave Quarters; Gilead Sher, negotiator for the Camp
David Summit and the Oslo Accords; and moderated
by Tim Phillips of Beyond Conflict.

Lyceum IV: New England Town Hall Meeting
October 16, 2016
Featuring: The public, Pedro Alonzo, Sam Durant;
moderated by Mary Jane Jacob, curator and writer.

Build Therefore Your Own World

**Blum & Poe, Los Angeles, California
January 7–February 18, 2017**

*"Every spirit builds itself a house, and beyond its house
a world…Build therefore your own world,"* 2017
Wood, vinyl text
$167\frac{1}{2}×539\frac{3}{4}×377$ in overall (425.5×1371×957.6 cm)
Fabricators: Ross Caliendo, Michael Dodge, Aaron
Freeman, Norm Laich, Josh Rubens, Sam Scharf,
Ben Carlton Turner, and Lowell Wilson

*Erasure, Appearance (Garrison's Walking Stick,
Thoreau's Pencil)*, 2016
Bronze
$48\frac{7}{8}×4\frac{1}{4}×7\frac{3}{8}$ in (124.1×10.8×18.7 cm)
Fabricator: Dyson & Womack

Transcendental (Wheatley's Desk, Emerson's Chair), 2016
Painted wood
$53\frac{3}{4}×34\frac{1}{4}×34\frac{1}{2}$ in (136.5×87×87.6 cm)
Fabricator: Dyson & Womack

Fieldstones (after Robin Coste Lewis' Erasures), 2016
Bronze with patina
Six parts: $3\frac{1}{2}×10×6\frac{3}{4}$ in (8.9×25.4×17.1 cm); $3\frac{1}{2}×8×5\frac{7}{8}$ in
(8.9×20.3×14.9 cm); $4\frac{1}{4}×9\frac{1}{4}×6\frac{1}{2}$ in (10.8×23.5×16.5 cm);
$2\frac{3}{4}×7\frac{3}{4}×7\frac{1}{4}$ in (7×19.7×18.4 cm); $3\frac{1}{8}×10\frac{3}{4}×6\frac{5}{8}$ in
(7.9×27.3×16.8 cm); $4\frac{1}{4}×8\frac{1}{8}×7\frac{3}{4}$ in (10.8×20.6×19.7 cm)

Dream Map, Ursa Minor, 2016
Prison blanket, pennies, epoxy
61×81 in (154.9×205.7 cm)
Fabricator: Gloria Galvez

Dream Map, North Star, 2016
Prison blanket, pennies, epoxy
$78\frac{1}{2}×42\frac{1}{2}$ in (199.4×108 cm)
Fabricator: Gloria Galvez

Dream Map, Polaris, 2016
Military blanket, pennies, epoxy
63×74 in (160×188 cm)
Fabricator: Gloria Galvez

Race Traitor, 2016
Carbon steel
$14\frac{1}{8}×1\frac{3}{8}×1\frac{3}{8}$ in (35.9×3.5×3.5 cm)

Keep a Top Eye Open, Black Lives Matter, 2016
Archival digital print
25¾ × 18⅛ in (65.4 × 46 cm)

"God wills us free" (John Jack's Epitaph, Thoreau's Flute), 2016
Sandstone and bronze
31 × 21 × 14 in (78.7 × 53.3 × 35.6 cm)
Fabricator: Dyson & Womack

All artworks unique.

Build Therefore Your Own World Programming

Transformative Poetics and Music for Social Justice
January 27, 2017
Featuring: Authors Tisa Bryant, Robin Coste Lewis, and
Will Alexander reading new and recent work; and a solo
piano recital by composer/performer Donal Fox.

Contributors

Pedro Alonzo is a Boston-based independent curator, as well as an Adjunct Curator at Dallas Contemporary. Alonzo has contributed to various publications including the exhibition catalog *Keith Haring 1978–1982* (2010), and he edited and wrote for *Art and Agenda: Political Art and Activism* (2011). Alonzo has specialized in producing exhibitions that transcend the boundaries of the museum walls and spill out onto the urban landscape, intentionally addressing audiences beyond the traditional museum public. His recent exhibition and outdoor projects include *Adriana Varejão: Kindred Spirits*, Dallas Contemporary; *Open Source: Engaging Audiences in Public Space*, Philadelphia Mural Arts Program; and *Art and The Landscape*, a series of public art projects for The Trustees.

Tisa Bryant's writing thrives where genre, form, and subjectivity intersect. She is the author of *Unexplained Presence* (2007), a collection of fiction essays on Black presences in film, literature and visual arts; co-editor of the *Encyclopedia Project*, a cross-referenced literary journal; and a commissioned writer/researcher for Clockshop's *Radio Imagination*, the year-long Los Angeles celebration of science-fiction writer Octavia Butler. She is working on *The Curator*, a book of imagined cinema and lived experience, and *Residual*, an exploration of grief, longing, desire and archival research. She teaches writing at the California Institute of the Arts, and lives in Los Angeles.

Danielle Legros Georges was named Poet Laureate of the City of Boston in 2015, and is the author of two books of poems, *The Dear Remote Nearness of You* (2016) and *Maroon* (2001). She is Professor in the Creative Arts in Learning Division of Lesley University, Cambridge, MA, and a faculty member of the William Joiner Institute Summer Writer's Workshop, University of Massachusetts, Boston, Massachusetts. She serves as a consulting poetry editor for *Solstice* and *Salamander* literary magazines, and has curated poetry activity for exhibitions including the Institute of Contemporary Art, Boston's Black Mountain College exhibition *Leap Before You Look* (2015–16). Her honors include fellowships from the Massachusetts Cultural Council, the Boston Foundation, and commissions from The Trustees of Reservations and the Boston Public Library.

Robin Coste Lewis' first poetry collection, *Voyage of the Sable Venus*, won the National Book Award for poetry in 2015. She has been a finalist for the International War Poetry Prize, the National Rita Dove Prize, and a semifinalist for the "Discovery"/Boston Review Prize and the Crab Orchard Series Open Poetry Prize. Her work has appeared in the *Massachusetts Review*, *Callaloo*, the *Harvard Gay & Lesbian Review*, *Transition*, and *VIDA*, among others. She has taught at Wheaton College, Chicago, Illinois; Hunter College, New York, New York; Hampshire College, Amherst, Massachusetts; and the NYU Low-Residency MFA in Paris, and has received numerous residency fellowships and awards. Currently a Provost's Fellow at the University of Southern California, Lewis now lives in Los Angeles; her family is originally from New Orleans.

Tim Phillips is a pioneer in the field of conflict resolution and reconciliation, and CEO and co-founder of Beyond Conflict, a global non-profit initiative founded in 1992. Using the unique approach of "shared experience," Beyond Conflict helped catalyze the field of transitional justice and is internationally recognized for contributions to peace and reconciliation in several countries including Northern Ireland, El Salvador, South Africa, and Cuba. He has advised the United Nations, the US Department of State, and the Council of Europe on democracy and conflict resolution initiatives. Phillips also helped launch and serves on the Advisory Committee of the Club of Madrid, a forum for former democratic heads of state and government. Phillips serves on the board of directors of several cultural and educational institutions including the Museum of Fine Arts, Boston, the Rose Art Museum, Waltham, Massachusetts, and the Smithsonian Museum of Natural History, Washington DC.

Kevin Young is the author of eleven books of poetry and prose including *Blue Laws: Selected & Uncollected Poems 1995–2015* (2016), longlisted for the National Book Award, and *Book of Hours* (2014), a finalist for the Kingsley Tufts Poetry Award and winner of the Lenore Marshall Prize for Poetry from the Academy of American Poets. Young's *The Grey Album: On the Blackness of Blackness* (2012) won the Graywolf Press Nonfiction Prize and the PEN Open Book Award; it was also a *New York Times* Notable Book for 2012 and a finalist for the 2013 National Book Critics Circle Award for criticism. In December 2016, Young assumed the Directorship of the Schomburg Center for Research in Black Culture in New York.

The Meeting House / Build Therefore Your Own World

Published on the occasion of the following exhibitions by Sam Durant:

The Meeting House
Curated by Pedro Alonzo, commissioned by The Trustees
The Old Manse, Concord, MA
August 13–October 31, 2016

Build Therefore Your Own World
Blum & Poe, Los Angeles, CA
January 7–February 18, 2017

Director of Publications
Nicoletta Beyer

Contributors
Pedro Alonzo
Tim Phillips
Tisa Bryant
Danielle Legros Georges
Robin Coste Lewis
Kevin Young

Graphic Design
Chris Svensson

All artworks: © the artist.

Dust jacket
Sam Durant, *"Every spirit builds itself a house, and beyond its house a world... Build therefore your own world,"* 2017

Cover
Detail of Durant's *"Every spirit builds itself a house, and beyond its house a world...Build therefore your own world,"* 2017, featuring an excerpt of Danielle Legros Georges' poem "Walden Woods."

Photo credits
All Concord, MA, photography: Above Summit, courtesy The Trustees, except 2, 4, 8, 10 (fig. 9), 11 (figs. 12, 13), 12 (fig. 15), 18–21, 28–31, 96: Alex Jones, courtesy The Trustees.

All Los Angeles, CA photography: Joshua White/ JWPictures.com.

Other images: Installation view at Los Angeles County Museum of Art, 2014, © Museum Associates/LACMA: 6 (fig. 2); photo: John Paul Doguin, courtesy Bakalar & Paine Galleries, Massachusetts College of Art and Design: 6 (fig. 3); photo: Steve Weinik for the City of Philadelphia Mural Arts Program: 7 (fig. 4); reproductions courtesy Concord Free Public Library: 10 (fig. 10), 29 (no. 6); Collection of the Massachusetts Historical Society: 11 (fig. 11); archival reproductions courtesy the Library of Congress: 28 (nos. 1, 3).

Acknowledgments
The Meeting House and *Build Therefore Your Own World* would have been impossible without the unwavering support of many people. I am indebted to curator Pedro Alonzo for his commitment and dedication. I am deeply appreciative of The Trustees' Art and The Landscape Committee—Stephanie Benenson, Karen Conway, Fotene Demoulas, Cindy Reed, Hope Suttin, Gail von Metzsch, and their innovative President Barbara Erickson. I am extremely grateful to Jeff Poe and Tim Blum, who have been supporting my work through thick and thin for more than twenty years. It was an honor to work with the architect/social justice team of Teddy Cruz and Fonna Forman, along with Armando Plata who ensured that the pavilion structure soared gracefully while withstanding a tornado. The fact that the sun shone radiantly on every event held at *The Meeting House* is fitting testament to Ena Fox's marvelous stewardship of the lyceums and public programming. Elizabeth Keary Soule, the Art and The Landscape Project Manager, supervised all aspects of *The Meeting House* with grace and humor. Special thanks to The Old Manse site manager Tom Beardsley, for his guidance and enthusiasm. Elise Lemire's *Black Walden* was foundational, her support and guidance crucial. Tim Phillips' emphasis on empathy and interconnectedness was transformational. I'm honored and inspired by four extraordinary poets: Kevin Young, Danielle Legros Georges, Robin Coste Lewis, and Tisa Bryant. Krista Buecking thoughtfully and carefully oversaw research and administration. I am thankful for Nicoletta Beyer's passion and care in steering this publication to completion, and Chris Svensson's talent for capturing the many facets of this project now articulated in print. Chris and Emily of Dyson & Womack, and Gloria Galvez, along with Michael Smoler, Benjamin Carlton Turner and Michael Dodge at Blum & Poe, allowed the production, exhibition, and publication of this work to blossom.
—*Sam Durant*

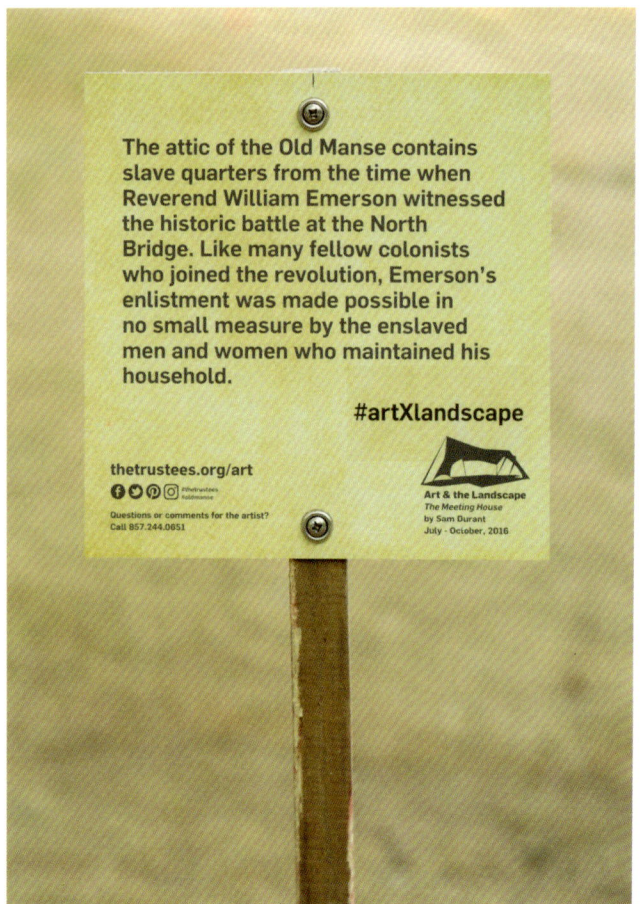

The attic of the Old Manse contains slave quarters from the time when Reverend William Emerson witnessed the historic battle at the North Bridge. Like many fellow colonists who joined the revolution, Emerson's enlistment was made possible in no small measure by the enslaved men and women who maintained his household.

#artXlandscape

thetrustees.org/art

Questions or comments for the artist? Call 857.244.0651

Art & the Landscape
The Meeting House
by Sam Durant
July - October, 2016

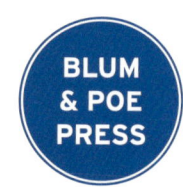

BLUM & POE PRESS

art design fashion
history photography
theory and things

black dog publishing

www.blackdogonline.com   london uk

Sam Durant